SCENES FROM THE PAST

BOLTON

- ENGINEMAN -

FOOTPLATE REFLECTIONS OF SHED LIFE & JOURNEYS FROM THE LANCASHIRE TOWN

"Shovelling for Steam"

A photograph full of nostalgia and some intrigue. Purely by chance, the photographer has captured a somewhat suspicious looking Jim Markland on board Black Five No **45200** of Fleetwood shed just as the train is leaving Bolton Trinity Street's platform 4. Everything points to this being the 3.50p.m to Liverpool. The class of engine is correct and from a shed which often supplied the power via a Lostock Hall diagram. However, the hands of the town hall clock decree it to be the 9.50a.m departure for Liverpool Exchange, usually the preserve of a Stanier 2-6-4 tank. In the background, Black Five No **45243** enters the station yard with an Up express. The date is Thursday, September 3rd 1964.   *H. L. Holland*

JIM MARKLAND

Copyright © 1997 Foxline Publishing and Jim Markland
ISBN 1 870119 49 5
All rights reserved
Edited by G. K. Fox
Feature Designs and Layout by Stuart Taylor
Typeset by W. G. Rear and G. K. Fox
Printed by Amadeus Press, Huddersfield
Published by Foxline Publishing, 32 Urwick Road,
Romiley, Stockport, SK6 3JS

Young Jim Markland at age 14, a photograph taken professionally for inclusion in the programme for Bolton Amateur Operatic Society on the occasion of its Diamond Jubilee presentation of Ivor Novello's musical "The Dancing Years" during December 1955, at the Theatre Royal, Bolton. The seven performances were certainly a memorable experience, but it was the footplate and not the footlights where my future career lay.
Author's collection

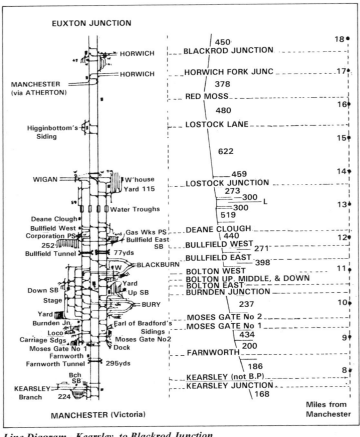

Line Diagram - Kearsley to Blackrod Junction

Contents

Chapter 1............Gateway to the future......................5
Chapter 2............Errands to Horwich.......................12
Chapter 3............Shed life at Bolton in the 1950's......16
Chapter 4............That first firing turn - on 49544......23
Chapter 5............Firing the old man's link................26
Chapter 6............Firing turn No 4 - 40072
　　　　　　　　　　- to Rochdale and back..................32
Chapter 7............Yorkshire coal for Liverpool
　　　　　　　　　　(first main line freight turn............34
Chapter 8............Willing workhorse, the "Crabs".......52
Chapter 9............Days out on Derby 4's..................62
Chapter 10..........Ivatt 4's (Ironhorses)....................66

Chapter 11..........The lighter side of shed life
　　　　　　　　　　at Bolton...................................73
Chapter 12..........Bolton No 2 passenger link...........77
Chapter 13..........The railmotor to Horwich.............81
Chapter 14..........Stanier Class Eights' on
　　　　　　　　　　passenger workings...................92
Chapter 15..........Passenger turns at Bolton
　　　　　　　　　　in the 1960's............................98
Chapter 16..........Passing out parade
　　　　　　　　　　(Driving exam - March 1965....103
Chapter 17..........A changing world
　　　　　　　　　　- Steam twilight at Bolton.........105

October 1st 1957. B.R. Standard 2-6-0 Class 4 No.**76080**, belonging to Lower Darwen shed, hurries past Bolton shed on an express working to Manchester Victoria. In the background is Burnden Junction's Down signal gantry, whilst the signalbox itself is just visible to the right of the parachute water column. Two locomen are making their way back to Bolton shed to sign off duty, the one on the right is fireman Bill Buchannan. Some years later Bill left the footplate and took up duties as steamriser at the shed. *Colin Boocock.*

Acknowledgements

In compiling this book, about my days at Bolton M.P.D., I have been fortunate to have had the help, advice and assistance of the following people to whom I give grateful thanks. Steve Leyland for his painstaking research, Stuart Taylor for feature designs and layout of the book. Derek Ralphs for his help with picture and publicity. Phil Vaughan for proof reading and lastly Bill Rear for his work in typesetting etc. Thanks also to the following "cameramen", without whom this volume would be sadly lacking in illustrations. Les Allen, Brian Barlow, Peter Baughan, Colin Boocock, B.F.I. Stills dept., the archives of Bolton Evening News, and Bolton Wanderers F.C., Paul Claxton, Jim Davenport, the late Frank Dean, Peter Fitton, David Hampson, Bert Holland, J. Houghton, R. Horrocks, Steve Leyland, Bart Van Der Leeuw, Brian E. Morrison, Roy Panting, John E. Porter, Paul Salveson, Chris Spring, M.S. Stokes, Bert Welsby. Official pictures of Bolton and Horwich by British Railways and the NRM.

I thank also the following Bolton locomen for their help in piecing together some of the workings and details relating to Bolton M.P.D. in the 1950's & 60's. George "Tag" Ashworth, Bob Collier, Bob Croston, Tommy Crook, Wilf Faulkner, Malcolm Frost, Ronnie Horrocks, Jimmy Jones, Bill Martin, Tommy Moore, Ken Roberts, Joe Strickleton, Granville Walmsley and Bert Welsby.

The nerve centre at Crescent Road Motive Power Depot, the Running Shift Foreman's office, where details of the extra power needed in order to cope with increased traffic demands during the "Wakes Holiday" are being recorded by Running Shift Foreman Jim Openshaw and his assistant Rowland Hill. On top of the switchboard, next to the "National" telephone is the board showing which roads the engines are stabled on, above Mr. Hill's head is the rack containing time cards, and further to the right, shelving with drivers' dockets, detailing their days work. By Mr. Hill's elbow is stacked a pile of driver's weekly notices. The date on the calendar is June 27th, whilst the year is 1950. *Author's collection.*

BOLTON ENGINEMAN
- Introduction -

During the 1950's, the landscape around Bolton was vastly different to that of more recent times. There was a great deal of Industry and the town was surrounded by cotton mills, their chimneys constantly belching thick smoke into the atmosphere. The coal fired power stations of Halliwell and Kearsley also contributed to the "clag", and from those cooling towers, the billowing clouds of steam would drift forever skyward. As a child of ten in 1950, I could see from our family smallholding on a hillside of Harwood, plenty of activity on the railway. It was like a magnet, and when the wind came from the south-west the sounds could also be heard from the Bolton to Blackburn line. Standing on our garden wall, I could see and hear, in the distance, the bank engine at Bradshawgate, whistling at the rear of freight trains that it was ready to assist over the next seven difficult miles up to Entwistle. On occasions, a "breather" at The Oaks would ensue, to let a passenger train overtake it. From that point onwards, I could watch it as far as Turton & Edgworth before losing it amongst the hills. During school holidays, I could also watch what for me was a most stirring sight, as the Colne to London express, with its eight corridor coaches, finished in "strawberries and cream", sped through The Oaks at about sixty miles an hour,

behind a Black Five, whistling a warning at the crossing, each day about ten minutes past nine. As if that were not enough, I attended two senior schools close by the railway. Undoubtedly, some of the foregoing must have influenced my choice of career in that December of 1955, but I didn't really think about it at the time. In recording in this volume some of those happenings of forty or so years ago, I have sought to illustrate what life was like at a running shed and on the footplate. Both were crude, dirty workplaces, and whilst footplate work called for a high degree of responsibility, there were moments when both humour and tragedy were encountered.

Working on the railway and being involved with the many characters portrayed in this book gave me, and many others, a unique insight into a way of life which was destined for sudden change in the fast moving nineteen sixties. As a result, I consider myself to have been fortunate in having taken part in the final days of Bolton's "steam era". I wouldn't have missed it for the world!

Jim Markland
St Annes on Sea; Lancashire
July 1997

On August 25th 1955, motor fitted "radial" tank No **50660** is ready to have its bunker topped up after working the afternoon Horwich to Blackrod motor service. This loco along with sister engine No 50647 shared the working during the later 1950's until 50660 was withdrawn in March 1958, and the arrival in April of the same year of BR Standard 2-6-2T No 84019. *Brian E. Morrison*

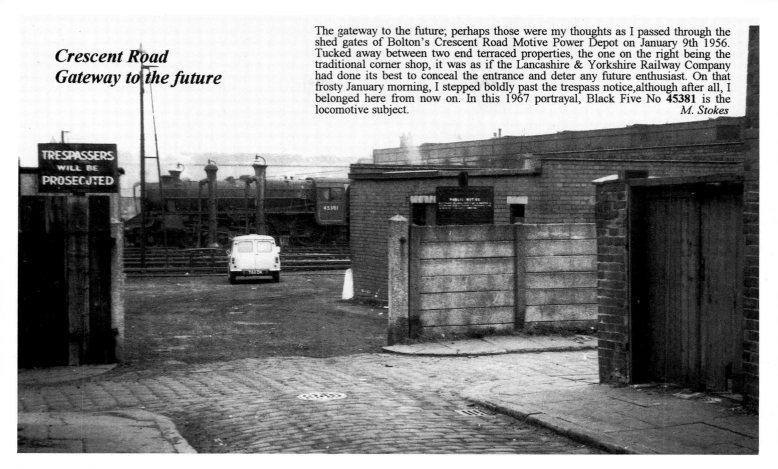

**Crescent Road
Gateway to the future**

The gateway to the future; perhaps those were my thoughts as I passed through the shed gates of Bolton's Crescent Road Motive Power Depot on January 9th 1956. Tucked away between two end terraced properties, the one on the right being the traditional corner shop, it was as if the Lancashire & Yorkshire Railway Company had done its best to conceal the entrance and deter any future enthusiast. On that frosty January morning, I stepped boldly past the trespass notice, although after all, I belonged here from now on. In this 1967 portrayal, Black Five No **45381** is the locomotive subject.
M. Stokes

Chapter One

Just before leaving school in December of 1955, I had paid a visit to the Youth Employment Officer, the purpose being to determine my future career.

I told him that I wanted to work on the railway.

"Which part of the railway"?

"On the engines", I said.

At this point, my mother, who had accompanied me at the meeting, became somewhat agitated, expressing her opinion that this was not the safest of occupations.

However, the official arranged an interview with the Shedmaster at Bolton Motive Power depot later that month, where an informal eyesight test took place. The latter was satisfactory, but I was told that I would need to have a medical examination by the railway's own doctor in Manchester and a more formal sight test. I came away from the interview at Bolton Shed knowing that my railway career was almost assured, walked out of the bosses front door, which I closed behind me, and its brass knob came away in my hand. I was somewhat embarrassed. As I hurriedly tried to mend the broken appendage a sudden thought crossed my mind, perhaps I ought to join the fitting staff! The formalities of medical and eyesight test took place early in January of 1956, there were no problems. I was told to report for work at Bolton Motive Power Depot on January 9th, 1956 at 8.00am. I had become an engine cleaner, the first rung on the ladder of the footplate fraternity. By 8.00am of that frosty morning in 1956, all seven or eight of the cleaning gang had arrived and signed on in the Running Shift Foreman's Office, each of us receiving a metal check with our number stamped on it. Some of the gang were sat on the bench seat which ran almost the full length of the office. Others, including myself, as new recruits were coming to terms with the "*Shops,Offices:& Railway*

Premises Act" displayed in the notice case behind the seat. Eventually, Len, the Foreman Cleaner, came from his office to tell us which engines we were to clean. We all followed him out on to number 1 road. Four of us were nominated to clean the engine standing dead at the top of number 4 road, Len pointing us in its direction, **52132**, which was in process of having its boiler washed out. Being the youngest hand on our gang, I was "volunteered" to go to the stores to draw out a bucket of cleaning oil, some sponge cloths and scrapers to get the grime off the side rods and motion parts. Now **52132** was a pretty old specimen, for as train spotters - I was never an avid one, we knew them as "Coffee Pots". As railwaymen they were "A" Classes, actually an 0-6-0 goods engine of the Lancashire & Yorkshire Railway first introduced in 1889. In their original form they carried a round topped firebox,but some, including this one, had been rebuilt with a Belpaire boiler and firebox. Because of the new shape of the firebox they were sometimes referred to as "Square Faced A Classes", especially by some of the older railwaymen. Although **52132** had received its British Railways number by this time, its tender still bore evidence of a former ownership,the letters **L.M.S** standing out boldly in large though somewhat tarnished yellow. We set to work, four of us, and completed the cleaning of one side of the engine in double quick time, then retired to the "cabin"or mess room for a brew. We were promptly turfed out by Len on one of his regular trips around the shed to see what we were doing. He also asked somewhat sarcastically was the other side of the engine not going out of the shed as we had not cleaned it. On this occasion we were using cleaning oil, but periodically a delivery of "A" cleaning solution would arrive in forty gallon barrels, which had to be used until the supply was exhausted. I can best describe the solution as a white liquid of chemical content which was applied to the engines paintwork with long handelled brushes, then swilled off with water.

"Go an' clean that 'tea pot' at 'top o' number four road, No 52132". That was the introduction to cleaning duties from the foreman cleaner, Len Yarwood, on Monday January 9th, 1956. Depicted in this August 1955 scene, No **52132** is as described in the main text, still with the legend LMS on the tender as bold as brass. This Belpaire rebuild of 1910 lasted until March 1957 when she was scrapped at Horwich Works. Driver Joe Axford is at the controls, his brother Jim at the time being Leading Fitter, later becoming Shedmaster.
Brian E. Morrison

Although it had the desired effect of cleaning the paintwork, it never left the shine of the cleaning oil and was of no use on motion parts or wheels. As engine cleaners we got up to all sorts of tricks. A new recruit would be busy cleaning away at some part of the smokebox when one of the gang, nominated by the group, would tell the new recruit not to forget the inside of the chimney. Minutes later, the foreman cleaner would arrive on the scene and would want to know what the culprit was up to. Another favourite trick would be for one of the gang to drop his lighted cigarette end into an unsuspecting cleaners pocket. As a cleaner on the receiving end, I can personally vouch for this one, the first you knew of the prank was a strange pricking sensation about waist level. Closer examination revealed a large hole in the slop jacket pocket, with volumes of smoke issuing from the offending area. At some distance, the rest of the gang could be seen doubled up with laughter at the sight of an engine cleaner on fire, making frantic efforts to put out the blazing pocket. The "cabin" or mess room on number one road frequently was a "mess", and periodically, the bench seats and tables would be dragged out by the side of number one road and the place then given a thorough going over. The concrete floor was swept and the place mopped out with scalding hot water and soda ash, then swilled out with the power hose used by the boiler men when washing out loco boilers. Occasionally, the mopping out process was omitted by the cleaning gang looking for a bit of fun. Two or three of them would get together, grab the power hose, switch on the power pump, couple up the hose to the nearest hydrant and then turn on the water to full force. Bursting into the cabin, they would unceremoniously hose it down together with the recumbent occupants, violent recriminations often followed. The chimney from the fireplace in the messroom was a persistent source of trouble, it was often blocked with soot. A "volunteer" from the cleaning gang was sought and coerced into getting on to the roof of the cabin armed with a can of paraffin, the liquid was then poured unceremoniously down the chimney almost cremating the inhabitants, rather too much of the potent brew having been dispensed. An alternative to the foregoing was again for a "volunteer" to climb on to the roof and drop a couple of detonators down the chimney. This always cleared soot and the cabin as well and was often done just as a prank. In addition to being a place where staff ate their food, the mess room was used when one wanted a snooze. After eating lunch, or as was often the case, supper, during the night shift. Some of the shed staff, including engine cleaners, put a bench seat end on to the wall by the fire and had a sleep. One particular Saturday night, the shedman, whose job it was to keep the ash pit emptied had indulged in such a snooze. Being Saturday night he'd "had a few" and fell asleep. Such was his condition that we were able to stick the boiler washers hose pipe inside the leg of his overalls and then turn on the water with obvious results. The Foreman Cleaner - there were two of them, one on the 8.00am turn, and the other one on the midnight turn - had a difficult time of it trying to keep us working. We knew them by the name "Cruelty Man". No sooner had he turned his back and we would be off skiving somewhere over the other side of the shed. Often a card school would be in progress. Favourite places would be a warm footplate out of the way, the sandhole or even the cabin. If the "early warning" system failed and we were caught playing cards, the offending pack would be confiscated and a firm lecture given, usually in the bosses "front office". Often, threats of "Form One's" being issued were delivered to those indulging in such past-times on the company's property, along with the possibility of the offence being entered on ones record of service. Frequently, the lure of an engine in steam proved too much of a temptation, and just sitting there, tinkering with the controls was a favourite pastime. Alas, "Cruelty Man" knew all our haunts and all too soon we were sent back to our cleaning duties. On the afternoon, 4.00pm shift there wasn't actually a foreman cleaner on duty, the telephone attendant who signed on at that time took it upon himself to see to those cleaners who would be going off duty at 5.00pm, he also supervised the passed cleaners on duty during his shift. Occasionally, the regular Running Shift Foreman, the one who arranged the power for the various jobs and arranged for the engines to be shedded in the correct order, and either engine or tender first off the shed, would have a day off, a "deputy" covering his duty." Deputies" were locomen specially trained for this work and would take their turn on such occasions. One particular afternoon with one of the deputies, Bill Liddle, on duty, he walked into the cabin where a card school was in progress. Bill was a witty soul and asked us cleaners just what we were up to. One of our number replied that we were engine cleaning, whereupon Bill retorted that we must have bloody long arms, since number 4 road where we were supposed to be was a good twenty yards away. Engine cleaning was a thoroughly filthy job, some engines not having been cleaned for a month, and the grime on the side rods might be a quarter of an inch thick. Most of the dirt seemed to get transferred to ones overalls, and it didn't help matters when gang warfare broke out amongst the cleaning gangs. The "ammunition" was oil soaked cleaning cloths. You were devastated when one struck you fair and square to the side of your face. One of the dirtiest jobs, often undertaken by a cleaner was the "Bar Lad". At the time of which I write, 1956, cleaning rate of pay was £3.4.0d, or in todays money, £3.20 per week. Of this, your take home pay was £3 and one penny for a five and a half day week. The Bar Lad was paid at labouring rate of pay and could therefore, draw about £7 for a full weeks work, so there were usually plenty of volunteers. When an engine came on shed for its periodical boiler washout and exam, fourteen days for a passenger engine and about twenty eight days for a freight loco, the fire was thrown out in the ash pit and the engine stabled on number four road where the steam was blown down and the engine's boiler and firebox allowed to cool. Some hours later, usually on the 8.00am shift, the Bar Lad, suitably equipped with protective clothing and face mask to guard against the dust and ash, would squeeze into the firebox via the firehole doors. In order to help him see inside the firebox, he would have with him a carbide lamp, fuelled with crystals of carbide of calcium, which, when water was added, produced a gas and when burned under controlled conditions in these lamps produced a smokeless flame, so ideal for use in confined spaces, such as an engine's firebox. His was now the unenviable job of cleaning all the clinker from the firebox,tubeplate, brick arch and the renewing of any badly burned firebars. In process of this work you got thoroughly filthy, and two or three engines a day were quite enough to deal with. I was never asked to do the Bar Lad's job, and really, I was quite glad about that. Instead, my job, after about three months cleaning engines was looking after the sandhole. On a steam engine, sand is an essential commodity in order for the driving wheels to get a good grip on a greasy or wet rail. Before the sand could be put into the sand boxes (sanders) on an engine, it had to be dried so that it would flow more easily, hence the need for the sand drying furnace. Periodically, a wagon of wet sand would arrive at the shed, about three or four tons. It would eventually be positioned outside the sandhole on the shed loop, the brake pinned down and then the wagon would be emptied, usually by a couple of cleaners. In the centre of the sandhole was the "Kelbus" or sand drying furnace. This was mounted over sloping metal screens which allowed the dry sand to pass through into the pit below. From there it was conveyed by wheelbarrow to the two sandbins in the shed, one on number five road and the other on number nine road. From these bins the sand would be collected by firemen in a bucket with a special long nozzle,as part of engine preparation duties before leaving the shed for the days work. As Bolton was the running-in depot for most engines either built or repaired at

Horwich Loco Works there was plenty of demand for dry sand. Each engine had either four or six sanders, each of them would require filling and would take two or three buckets of dry sand to fill them, they were usually empty ex works. Engine cleaners were often employed filling them as they arrived because of the extra time that would have been involved during the limited preparation time a fireman had at his disposal. Some weeks, seven or eight engines would arrive from Horwich for trialling. This could increase during the period immediately before the Bolton and Horwich holiday fortnights, as many as possible being returned to traffic to cope with the extra power demand.

High up on top of Bolton's coaling plant looking in the direction of the town. Stanier Black Five No.**45061** of Southport is coming on to shed for loco duties mid morning, some time around 1959. In the left background is the engineering factory of Entwistle & Gass, just behind the vacuum operated turntable. Burnden Junction's Down signal gantry is just visible top right. *Author.*

A September 1964 arrival from Blackpool, No.**44947** shunts an assortment of vacuum fitted vehicles into Burnden sidings during 1967. A brazier has been placed by the water crane to the right on the picture on the coal road and piles of ash beneath the brazier suggest recent use. The road in the foreground swinging sharply leftward leads to the turntable.
M. Stokes

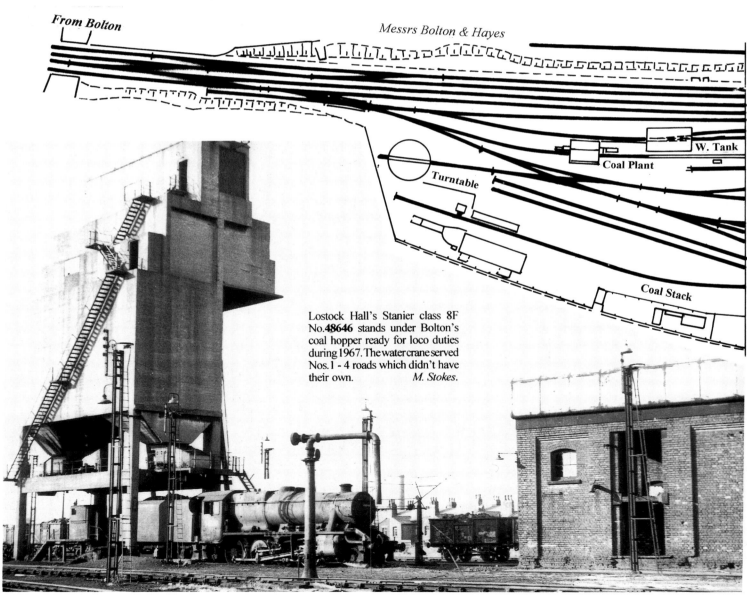

Lostock Hall's Stanier class 8F No.**48646** stands under Bolton's coal hopper ready for loco duties during 1967. The water crane served Nos.1 - 4 roads which didn't have their own.　*M. Stokes.*

Bolton MPD

Stanier class 8F No.**48652** on Number 1 road at Bolton shed is missing its snow plough in this portrayal. Standard Wagon Works on the other side of the main line. A small ground-frame named Bradford Siding facilitated entry into its private siding. No date for this view, but No.48652 was a Bolton engine from April 1965 until its withdrawal in June 1968.
J. Davenport.

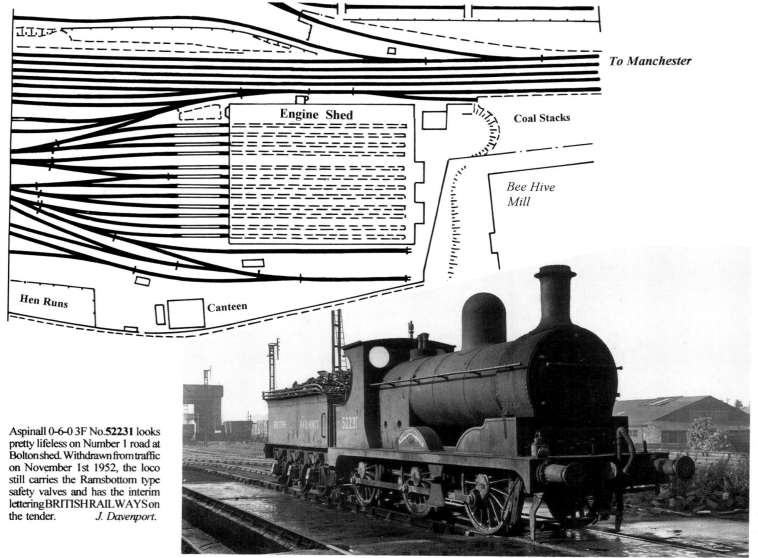

To Manchester

Engine Shed

Coal Stacks

Bee Hive Mill

Hen Runs

Canteen

Aspinall 0-6-0 3F No.**52231** looks pretty lifeless on Number 1 road at Bolton shed. Withdrawn from traffic on November 1st 1952, the loco still carries the Ramsbottom type safety valves and has the interim lettering BRITISH RAILWAYS on the tender.
J. Davenport.

(left)

Inside one of the cars of the Motive Power Instruction Train. Driver George Merry, (capless), Secretary of the Mutual Improvement Class (MIC), explains some of the finer points of loco work in front of the mock up of an ex LMS firebox faceplate and associated steam valves, boiler water gauge glasses, fire doors and main regulator valve. From the left are pictured, fireman Bert Welsby, George("Tag")Ashworth, Wilf Faulkner (kneeling) driver Merry,and driver (Frowzy) Fred Longworth. In addition to the mock up shown here, the instruction car contained working models of various types of valve-gear, driver's brake valves and cut away sections of valves and pistons also in model form, so it was possible to have a better understanding of the valve events on steam engine. The date of the photograph is Monday January 21st 1952.

Courtesy Bert Welsby

(below – left)

The "Mutual Improvement Class" committee members in the early 1950s, from left to right, driver George Merry, Footplate Inspector Jack Walkden, Fireman Bert Welsby, Driver Bill Croston, and former driver Fred Bullough, here representing shed staff. The occasion is that of the appointing of Bert Welsby as M.I.C. secretary.

Courtesy Bert Welsby

(below)

During the thirteen years the author spent as a locoman, there was only one occasion when union action was resorted to on a National scale, this in the form of a work to rule. Here though, a photograph taken during less contented times with the Bolton branch of A.S.L.E.F strike committee on view. On the back row, from the left, Passed Firemen T.Moore, K.Roberts, T.Jordan, Driver E.Rothwell & Fireman A.Chadwick. Centre left; just visible Driver J.Greenhalgh, Driver J.Axford, Driver J.Cornwell. Front row, left to right; Fireman T.Cocker, Passed Fireman W.Bridge, Fireman G.Hargreaves, Passed Fireman R.Collier and Drivers W.Croston and G.Merry.

Courtesy Bert Welsby

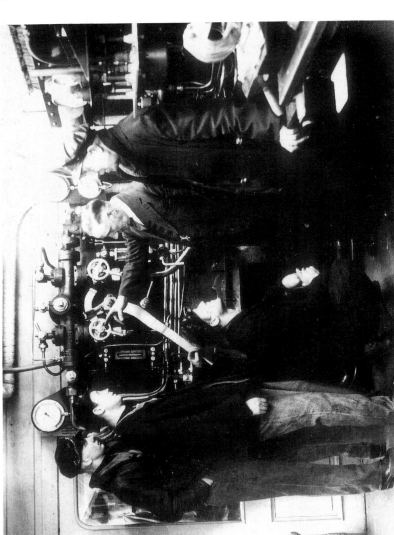

Bolton Shed Staff in the 1950's

Another 1950's photograph, this time of Bolton locomen along with their ladies. Although the exact date is not known, the gentleman on the back row on the extreme left is waving a small union flag, it is just possible that the photograph was taken during Coronation Year, 1953.

Courtesy Bert Welsby

In order to further ones understanding of footplate techniques, covering both driving and firing, there existed at Bolton an organisation known as the "Mutual Improvement Class", or just plain MIC for short. This 1947 photograph taken at Derby during a visit by Bolton enginemen to the works there conveys the level of interest that existed in improving ones knowledge. Not everyone in the photo is identified, but from the left, rear row with pipe is Albert Longworth, Tommy Moore looking over the latter's shoulder, Harry Berry in raincoat, Ernie Rothwell in lighter coloured trilby, Harry Holmes white collar and tie and trilby, in the middle of photo, is the younger, though somewhat balding Jimmy Jones, five along to the right (middle row) is John Thornton, whilst fourth from the right rear row is Ted Brierley. Left front kneeling is Harold Blackburn, whilst second and third from the right kneeling are Bill Croston and George Merry. This Derby trip was a joint one between Crescent Road and Plodder Lane, Bolton, depots.   *Courtesy Bert Welsby.*

Errands to Horwich

Chapter Two

During the time I was occupied as sand dryer, I was often taken off this work and sent on a mission to Horwich Loco Works for spare parts for engines that were "stopped". These spare parts were not normally available in the stores at the shed. The parts would be comparatively light things such as a drivers brake valve, a brass bush for a part of the engine's valve gear, a particular steam pipe or, in one extreme case, a set of tube expanders. Ordered in the normal way from the works, these parts could be a day or two arriving, resulting in the engine being "stopped" for that period of time. Instead, it was much quicker to send me by bus to the works to bring back the parts to the shed, thus the engine was put back into traffic much more quickly. There was also a bonus for me, instead of a ride back to Bolton by bus, there was the exciting possibility of riding back on a works engine. I always enjoyed these trips out, and found the works yard an interesting place to visit, along with the various shops located within its boundaries. Occasionally, I would take a copper pipe to the copper shop to be brazed. Invariably, I would be told that it would be an hour or two before it would be ready for collection. This gave me the opportunity to wander round such places as the paint shop or the finished work area. Here, I could see what engines would be coming off the shops in the not too distant future. Peering into the gloom of the old Horwich running shed, I wondered what ex L&Y 2-4-2 tank No.**50621** was doing there rusting away. Little did I know at that time that she was soon to be restored to her former state as L&Y No.**1008** and Horwich works number **1**, a candidate for preservation. Looking at the scrap road near to the office where I had to have my requisition notes stamped I could see the engines which had failed to make it. These had the foreboding words "*CUT UP*" stencilled on their valances. On my very first visit in 1956, there were several ex L&Y classes all in various stages of dismantling. But the one I remember best of all on this first occasion was the boiler of No.**52575** lying on the ground, close to what had been the rest of the engine. This was one of the very last of the superheater A Classes, and on its smokebox it still bore evidence of its last home depot, 26C, Bolton. By far the most interesting places for me though were the erecting and repair shops. Very often, when I had to collect spares, these had to be obtained from the stores, or as it was known locally, the "Glory Hole" beneath the erecting shop. When this was the case, I always made it my business to walk through as much of this part of the works as possible, it was so fascinating. Here was a feast of engines in various stages of repair, all facing the same way, having entered the works yard engine first. In those early days I noticed certain words stencilled on the valances over the wheels, I wondered what "GEN" "INT" & "Casual" might mean. I soon found out that "GEN" meant that the engine was to have a General repair, or complete overhaul, which meant stripping everything right down to the main frames. "INT", or Intermediate, might involve removal of valve gear, side rods, pistons, wheels, spring gear and axle boxes which were then given the necessary attention whilst the boiler was left in place. Casual repairs were those of a comparatively minor nature, straightening a buffer plank, repairs to damaged spring gear, perhaps due to derailment, and occasionally, minor collision damage. On some visits, if I was lucky I might see the overhead cranes lifting an engine and moving it forward over the line of engines beneath, setting it down again further along the shop on to the traverser. Once this was done the engine could then be moved sideways, and by these means moved out of the erecting shop, through the massive doors out on to the track which ran by the side of the shop. Often at this point, the tender tank was added and coupled up, then, from there, one of the works shunters dragged the whole ensemble to the weighing machine where final adjustments would be made to ensure that the weight was evenly distributed on the wheels. These technicalities complete, the engine would be ready for painting, and it was shunted into the paintshop. There, it would receive several coats of paint and varnish and have its number and BR crest applied, ready to emerge, shining and resplendent. Once painting operations were complete, the engine was dragged outside the paintshop in preparation for steaming. The tender or water tank was filled at the water column and the engine was then taken to the coal stage for a supply of coal, usually of indifferent quality. Now this coal stage can best be described as functional but somewhat antequated when compared to our modern coal hopper at Bolton. Basically, it was a large covered platform some two or so feet higher than rail level, in the middle of which was a crane which was electrically powered and which could pivot around on its fixed base. There were several flat bottomed scoops or buckets which the attendent kept filled, ready for when an engine needed coaling, each scoop containing about three or four hundredweight of coal. The method was that each engine that required coal was placed in the correct spot by the coal stage, the hook on the crane was attached to the scoop which was then swung over the engines coal space. There then followed quite a bit of prodding and poking at the release catch on the scoop, usually with a shunters pole, the contents were then disgorged into the tender or bunker in a few seconds. Seldom did one ask for more than two or three scoops, some pretty coarse comments ensued if you did, it was the coal mans policy to have to fill as few scoops as possible, after all, it was going to be filled mechanically once it arrived at the next depot, usually Bolton. The coaling operation complete, the engine would then be shunted to one of the roads close by the superintendents office, a sufficient supply of water would be fed into the boiler ready for the engine to be steamed. Next, a supply of coal would be shovelled into the firebox around the grate area by the steamraiser. Several firelighters were then placed on a shovel, lighted, and placed on the firebox grate area. From this time it would be several hours before the fire had spread sufficiently for steam to be raised. Once this was accomplished, various steam tests were made by the small army of fitters. The engine was almost ready to move under its own steam. Up to this point, the engine had been moved about the works yard by one of the pilots, and of course only slowly. Before any running was attempted under its own power, the engine had to be got ready or prepared. This now involved the locomen stationed at Horwich for this purpose and the trialling of engines on the main line. A supply of oil was obtained from the stores and all the various oiling points were filled up. To the West of the works yard there ran a length of track several hundred yards long, and just inside the perimeter. By the side of the track there was a fence comprised of sleepers about six or seven feet high. Once the engine was ready, several fitters and the locomen would be on the footplate and the engine would be run to the length of track and thence up and down it backwards and forwards. The fitters would be on the footplating that surrounded the boiler or in the cab, looking or listening for all manner of leaks, blows or any irregularities in the engines exhaust. Occasionally, the engine would be put under heavy steam by partially applying the steam brake and opening the regulator rather wider than would be the case under normal running light engine. By doing this, any leaks or blows would be more readily exposed. This process was known as "board siding" for obvious reasons, and was a preliminary to main line running. After several trips up and down the board side, the engine was returned to the finished work area where any defects would eventually be put right. In due course, the engine would be trialled on the main line. One of the primary purposes for doing this was to ensure that all bearing surfaces were receiving proper lubrication and that they would not run hot once back in revenue earning traffic. This trial trip could be a short sharp run tender first to Adlington Junction, there the engine would be signalled into the sidings. Driver and fireman would then climb down out of the cab and feel all round the engines coupled axles, motion bearings and tender axles looking for any signs of heating problems. If all was well, the instruction to take the engine light to Bolton could be carried out, there the engine would spend some time running in on local work before returning to its home depot. Occasionally, a longer trip was the order of the day, where doubt existed about the axle bearings or some other mechanical part. This involved a short run tender first to Blackrod Junction on to the main line where the engine was reversed over the points, and now ran engine first, via Bolton, over the now lifted Johnson Street connecting line to Blackburn. There, the engine was again reversed and now ran tender first to Chorley over the now closed and lifted Heapey branch, and onwards from there to Horwich Fork Junction where a final reversal took place enabling the engine to re-enter the works yard engine first. During this trial, the crew might ask to be turned inside at any convenient point should there be an overheating problem. From then onwards it could be a case of returning to the works at slow speed in order to minimise any possible damage. On arrival back at the works, any defects would be reported and put right. These could be a variety of things, sticking steamchest or cylinder mud taps (relief cocks) were often a source of trouble, injectors that failed to work properly, or a stiff reversing wheel, these were just a few of possible problems encountered. During 1960 I was marked for a number of weeks work on the "trials" job which by this time had been moved to the "514" or spare link at Bolton. On one occasion whilst

firing on this turn, I had climbed on to the footplate of a "Crab" 2-6-0 in order to set it for oiling. As was the normal practice, I fully applied the engines steam brake in order to make taking off the tender hand brake more easy. Once I had done this, I opened the small ejector in order to create vacuum which would blow off the steam brake. I then put the engine into full back gear, opened the regulator, and the joint on the steam dome blew out. On another occasion, climbing on to the footplate of a Derby Four which had been in steam several hours, one thing I immediately noticed was, although the safety valves were sizzling nicely, indicating a pressure close to blowing off point there was nothing showing on the boiler pressure gauge. Closer examination revealed that a careless fitter had coupled the pipe which should have gone to the steam pressure gauge to the vacuum gauge and vice versa. Before the engine left the works for its next destination, a last minute job would be replacing or completing the floorboarding on the footplate. Eventually the "woodchoppers" arrived, three or four of them, armed with the necessary boards of the right length but which would require a certain amount of "tailoring". In their tool kit they carried extremely sharp axes. The speed and accuracy they displayed as they chamferred and shaped the edges of the boards in order to make them a snug fit had to be seen to be believed. Only a few minutes, literally, and the job was done. They departed as quickly as they came, off to their next job. In due course, once this and any other problems had been ironed out another "works" engine would make its way down the yard whistling for the signal at the West Gate box. There, word would be passed to the signalman where the engine was bound for, often light to Bolton via Blackrod Junction where reversal would take place to enable engine first running. So it was, on such a trip as this that I made my first journey on a steam engine, an engine cleaner collecting spares from the works. Back at Bolton shed, the spares were taken to the leading fitters office, and afterwards I was told to resume sand drying duties. Before going back to those duties, first of all knock on the small frosted glass window, behind which was the General Office. The window would be opened by an equally frosted looking clerk, from whom I would request an expense claim form because I had taken my meal away from the depot. After the clerk had enquired for what purpose I wanted the form he would suggest I book off half an hour early and go home, I stoutly would refuse, saying on whose instructions I was making the claim, he always backed down. The amount claimed - two shillings!

Horwich

A deserted Horwich station, n.d., just as I remember it. Passengers here were hard to come by, and those that used the station were, for the most part, railway employees. The rail motor stock was normally stabled on the line in the foreground next to the warehouse, a glimpse of which is just visible. *N. R. Knight.*

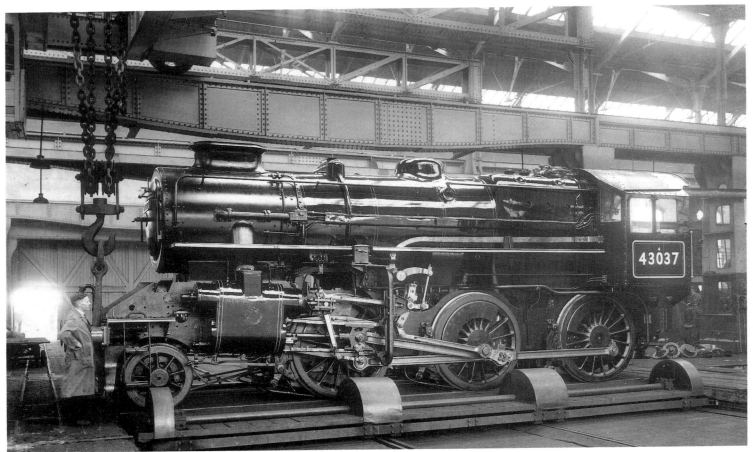

(opposite page - upper left)
By now a part of British Railways, Horwich is busy building the first batch of Ivatt 2-6-0's, numbered 43000-43049, all being supplied with double chimneys. One of the batch is being wheeled. Tenders for the new locos are visible on the other side of the erecting shop in this June 14th 1949 view.

(opposite page - lower)
The completed loco has been set down on the traverser by the overhead crane and will then be moved sideways, out of the erecting shop to take its place on the tracks outside **(this page - above)**. No **43037** will then be drawn forward by one of the Works shunter's off the traverser. The tender would be similarly brought out and the sections paired up.

(this page - right lower)
The Horwich coaling stage on April 8th 1963. The crane was electrically powered, and after attaching a loaded container of coal, could be pivoted around to position it's load exactly where required. Driver Walt Mather (back to camera), demonstrates what happened when he was involved in an accident with one of the coal buckets.

All: National Railway Museum

Chapter Three

Right from the earliest days of my railway career I loved driving steam engines, but as an engine cleaner this was, strictly speaking not allowed. There were however, ways and means that one could get to have a drive about the shed yard using a degree of caution. Working away at my sand drying duties, if I made a determined effort and got my work done, I could have the "Kelbus" (sand furnace) burning nicely, filled with wet sand and both of the bins in the shed filled with dry sand by 11.00am. It was much easier to sneak off this sort of work than it was from engine cleaning duties where the foreman cleaner could keep a watchful eye on the cleaning gang. Just about 11.15am, or not much later, the "Bank Shunt" engine would arrive back on the shed. The name "Bank Shunt" was actually taken from part of the engines diagram for the day. The engine, always an "Austin Seven" at this time, would have left the shed at 3.55am, and run light engine tender first to Brindle Heath Sidings to work the 4.50am goods job to Bullfield Down Sidings, just outside Bolton. Once the train had been shunted, the engine crossed over to the Up side into the sidings adjacent to where the gas works once stood. Here the the engine crew had their meal break in the shunters cabin, and afterwards the train for the "Bank Shunt"would be made up. This comprised of wagons for the various sidings all the way up the bank to Entwistle during my footplate days, hence the name "Bank Shunt". Leaving Bullfield at 8.10am and now running tender first over the now lifted Johnson Street connecting line, this trip and shunt portion of the job called at all sorts of odd places. Very occasionally it might put off a wagon or two of coal at Bradshawgate, but was not actually booked to do so. Usually its first port of call was Craddock Lane Down Side, to put off loaded coal wagons and take out empty ones from Fisks Siding. On the Up side, loaded wagons of steel would be left in the loop for Peers Steelworks. From there, the next port of call would be Bromley Cross, and it was approaching the latter that

as school kids we nicknamed this job the "ten to nine goods", as it made its way, often slipping heavily on the damp rail, up to the ground frame points at Bromley Cross North. Once clear of these points, the guard would operate the ground frame and the train was then propelled inside, clear of the main line ready for the passage of the 9.00am passenger train out of Bolton to Hellifield. After the passage of the Hellifield train, and once all its shunting movements had been carried out, Entwistle, near the top of the bank would be next call, and more shunting. Loaded wagons in, empties out. On the way back down the bank, Turton would receive a visit, a careful one, the lines by this time were not in a good state, so you moved about cautiously. There might be a need to call in again at Bromley Cross to complete shunting there, and certainly there would be empty steel wagons from Peers to work into Burnden, plus the loaded ones left in the loop to shunt in. By 11.15am, Burnden was the last port of call, and not long after that this fairly busy job had arrived back on shed. Now these "Austin Sevens" - we had three of them at the time - Nos.**49532, 49538 & 49544** were not fitted with vacuum equipment, and could not therefore be turned on our vacuum operated turntable other than by hand. On this particular job they usually arrived back on shed the wrong way round, so help in turning them was always appreciated. Here was where I would sneak off, help with the cleaning of the fire and the turning of the engine, and for that was given the privilege of driving the engine into the shed. Occasionally, it was possible to have a drive, or at least a ride on the footplate a little earlier than this. As noted previously, the shed loop passed right by the sandhole where I was working. So, provided I'd made a good start and got the fire in the sand drying furnace going, all I needed to do was wait for the shed shunt engine, which would be busy shunting the coal road, to come by and I would be ready to jump on.

Shed life at

Bolton

in the 1950,s

One of Bolton's motor fitted 2-4-2 Radial tanks is ready to move under the coal hopper. Water is falling from the dust quenching sprinkler system in the shute. On 12th July, 1958, No.**50647** has a little over six months of her life left.

At the opposite end of the shed yard was situated the gas house. When shunts had to be made over there, provided you remembered to duck down when passing the offices in the shed loop you were well away from officialdom. If you were seen however, a swift end to the escapade would ensue. It wasn't too bad if one of the small 2-6-2 passenger tanks of Stanier's design was being used, you had some cover, but with an 0-6-0 "A" Class you were soon discovered even though the engine crew did their best to hide you. Besides sand drying, there were other ways a cleaner might earn some extra money; one of these was working on the coal stack. Every now and then wagons of coal would arrive at the shed especially for stacking. This stacking of coal was to guard against sudden shortages, such as a coal miners strike or any other emergency. Although it was stacked for the best possible reasons, it did nothing to enhance the quality of the coal. What had been good Yorkshire steam coal with a high calorific content soon became little better than "Nutty Slack". I also suppose that a good deal of it disappeared into the back yards or gardens in nearby Crescent Road, security at the shed was not that strict. Another mucky job which a cleaner might be asked to do was to assist in clearing the sump hole on the ash pit. In order to make disposal of ashes from the ash pit more easy, there was at one end of the ash pit a grid of about six feet in length and almost the width of the pit itself. Beneath the grid several feet down there was constructed a shaft with a chamber or sump at the bottom. At the bottom of the shaft there was located a bucket of somewhat smaller proportions than the sump. When the bucket was filled with ash and clinker from engine fireboxes, and suitably quenched with water from the spray above, it could then be lifted electrically up the shaft by means of the winch and tipped automatically into the waiting empty wagons. Occasionally, the cavity around the bucket became clogged and had to be cleared. The bucket was left in the raised position, red flags placed before the sump, and then one descended into the depths by ladder to clear by hand and bucket all the ash and clinker down there. During the mid fifties Bolton did not posess a large fleet of engines of its own, nor were they anything out of the ordinary, typifying most ex L&Y depots. A couple of "Long Leggers" or "Gallopers" the LMS class 2P 4-4-0's, Nos. **40586 & 40681**. At this time, one of them could be seen on the 3.50pm stopping train from Bolton to Liverpool Exchange. For further passenger work there were thirteen Stanier passenger tanks of LMS origin, Nos. **42472, 42545, 42565, 42626, 42629, 42630, 42633, 42635, 42652-6**. In addition to these, one could add for passenger work the ex L&Y 2-4-2T's of class 2P, Nos. **50647, 50660, 50850, 50855** and **50887**. During the time I was at Bolton I never saw any of the latter class on anything but purely local work. Frequently, along with other members of this class, which varied from time to time, they were stored out of use, some of them having protective tarpaulin lashed around the chimney top. Some of them would be stored on the shed loop near to Beehive Mill, others at the end of a shed road. The first two mentioned were push and pull fitted, and, as only one was required for the Horwich rail motor job, the other was stored. Sometimes, one of the motor fitted variety was used on the station pilot at Bolton. As befitted these elderly machines, the station pilot was not a strenuous affair. As part of the diagram, the morning turn worked the 7.15am stopper to Horwich and made a similar trip in the reverse direction, arriving back in Bolton at about 8.30am. In the afternoon its routine took it light engine to Horwich Works to pick up a stores van which it propelled off the works, ready to be collected by a later working in Horwich station yard. From there it would then back on to three coaches and work the 4.54pm to Bolton calling at Lostock Junction. After its passengers had de-trained at Bolton, the stock was propelled into Byng Street carriage sidings and at a fairly leisury pace the engine would run light to Bolton shed to rest until 3.30am the following morning.

Various 2P 4-4-0's visited Bolton, but none stayed longer than four years, probably because the shed had too many turns over the hilly road to Blackburn and Hellifield for a large diameter wheeled 4-4-0 to be of much use to them. No.40681, with hybrid Fowler/Deeley tender dating from the 1939-45 period, with a Fowler tank mounted upon a Deeley frame, hence the gap of about 9 inches between the rear of the tank and the rear bufferbeam, there is no beading to the tank sides. No.**40681** stands out of use on Number 3 road at Bolton shed during 1958. Fireman "Nat" Gillard nearer to the tender, and driver Len Yates are passing the loco. *J.Davenport*

For goods work, there were the three "Austin Sevens", Nos.**49532, 49538 & 49544**, and ten Austerities, Nos. **90110, 90206, 90267, 90271, 90297, 90402, 90641, 90712, 90725 & 90729**, often these were referred to as "Tarboilers", they were so grimy. For local shunting work there were three ex L&Y 0-6-0 saddle tanks, Nos.**51486, 51511 & 51513**. To complete the picture, five ex L&Y "A Classes", Nos.**52132, 52139, 52237, 52348, & 52389**, the best of the bunch being a lifelong resident, No.**52348**. Of course, there were other members of the classes which made their home at Bolton. Some of them stayed on until the end of their lives, others were merely passing migrants and stayed but a little while. It can be seen from the foregoing fairly short list of Motive Power, that Bolton relied quite heavily on the trial engines from Horwich to fully meet its power demands. At this time, Horwich was repairing representatives from a variety of ex LMS, Midland and L&Y classes, and would shortly be building a further 25 BR Standard class four 2-6-0's, numbers **76075 - 76099**, the last new steam engines to be built there. Stanier class 3, 2-6-2 passenger tanks, for some reason we knew them by the name of "Breadvans" possibly on account of their small box like size. The Hughes Fowler Crabs, the Stanier straight framed or taper boilered Crabs. Ivatt class fours, nicknamed "Iron Horses" on account of the large amount of steel piping in them. Both Midland and LMS versions of the "Big Goods" 0-6-0's of class 4F visited Horwich, and it was a treat to work on Stanier class 8F's in ex works condition. Just occasionally, the odd "Austin Seven" would emerge having been given a light repair, but during 1957, General repairs were afforded to No.**49618** which was stripped right down to the frames. What a change to be able to work on an Austin that did not knock like a bag of bones. Very occasionally an ex L&Y "A" Class would emerge, some after a General overhaul, and more often than otherwise with Intermediate repairs, representatives of ex L&Y class "23", the 0-6-0 saddle tanks. A rare visitor would be the dock tanks of class 1F with their curious spark arresters which looked like a flying saucer in front of the chimney when not in use, and of course the 0-4-0 dock tanks of class 0F, referred to as "Pugs". In the case of the latter two varieties, if the engine was from a local shed, such as Aintree, Bank Hall or Agecroft, they went straight home from the works. Occasionally though, one of the ex L&Y 0-4-0 Pugs of class 0F would arrive at Bolton en route to its home depot at either Bristol or Goole. Because these little saddle tanks had such small wheels, they could travel only quite slowly when in steam. The usual practice therefore, was to throw the fire out on arrival at Bolton, the engine would then be put on to a convenient shed road. As soon as practical, the motionwork was then removed, the various parts being stowed away on any convenient part of the footplating. Once this operation had been completed, the loco was then able to be transported to its destination much as a wagon would be. One curious thing that happened when a loco had its side rods and connecting rods removed was that the crank-pins got out of sequence or alignment. In this state, we laughingly referred to them as "Freewheelers". Before much longer, there would be plenty of opportunities to work on almost all of these trial engines and a good many more. During October of 1956, the Loco Inspector and Motive Power Instruction Train paid a visit to Bolton in order to pass a number of us for firing duties. There were several sessions covering the Rule Book, with particular emphasis on Rule 55, the protection of trains. Added to this there were sessions covering firing techniques, and further instruction using the Instruction Car's facilities. Before we could start our firing duties there were further medical and eyesight tests to be

taken in Manchester, all necessary formalities. After all, we were now on the second rung of the ladder of the footplate fraternity. We'd "passed out", become passed cleaners, cleaners passed to act as firemen. Now our careers "Shovelling For Steam" could begin in earnest. Now that we had become passed cleaners, we had to work shifts, even though some of us were only sixteen. There were eight turns of duty for passed cleaners, and I always felt that the worst two were 4.00am for its sheer early start, and 6.00pm, this latter I always hated since most folks were on there way home from work at that time. Some of the other turns, 7.00am, 10.00am & 12.00 noon were most acceptable signing on times, and on the 3.00pm shift, you could at least get to bed at a normal hour. The other two turns, 9.00pm and midnight just had to be put up with. After signing on, one of the first topics of conversation would be discussing who was marked up for firing. Each day a daily alterations list was posted in the notice case. This showed which passed firemen were to sign on for driving, and which passed cleaners were to sign on for firing. It might also show which, if any, turns were cancelled. When those passed cleaners senior to oneself were marked up for firing, the excitement became intense. But it wasn't always so simple of course, you had to keep an eye on those on other shifts as well as your own turn. The reason for this was that when a passed cleaner was marked for firing duties, he could be moved three hours either side of his booked signing on time. From the foregoing, it is easy to see that if your signing on time was, say, 3.00pm, you would have to watch for those senior to yourself on the 12.00 noon turn, and also those on the 6.00pm shift being marked up before you stood a chance of a firing turn, and some extra cash. From time to time, a situation arose where you knew that if something unexpected occurred you would be wanted for firing. There might be a message from Control that the Tool Van or Breakdown Train was required to sort out a derailment. In this case the second most senior passed cleaner would be sent to relieve the most senior passed fireman on a nearby shunt job for driving duty. He would then walk back to the shed and with the senior passed cleaner would form the crew to work the Tool Van which was kept on number six road in the shed. Often, extra staff would be needed to man the Tool Van for breakdown work, especially in the early hours. Frequently, a passed cleaner would be despatched to the homes of the fitting staff to "knock them up", asking them to sign on immediately. When staff shortages were acute, though not very often, passed cleaners would be asked to make up the necessary numbers to enable the Tool Van to turn out. At Bolton, we were never able to deal with anything heavier than a wagon, so far as lifting was concerned. The hand operated crane which formed part of the ensemble, could only cope with about eight tons, and dated from the late nineteenth century. Another occupation a passed cleaner might be required to do was "Tooling". Usually this work was carried out during the 12.30 midnight shift since from that time forward until about 7.00am there would be the greatest number of locos leaving the shed. Very simply, the "Tool King" as he was known, had to make it his business to ensure that each and every engine due to go off shed that morning was "tooled up", had all its fire irons on board. From time to time, different instructions applied, depending on what equipment was left on the footplate after disposal. At one time or another headlamps, shovel, coal hammer and bucket containing gauge lamp, spanners and detonator cannister were left on board. Therefore, the "Tool King" had to make sure that these and the fire irons, paddle (or clinker shovel), pricker and dart, the latter usually used for loosening clinker under the door just

Bolton "Tar Boiler" 90712

Ministry of Supply Austerity 2-8-0 No. **90712** operates the Normanton to Manchester Victoria parcels train past Droylesden Junction on May 18th 1958. In January 1956, along with, Nos. 90110, 90206, 90267, 90271, 90297, 90402, 90641, 90725 and 90729, this loco was a Bolton engine before moving to Aintree in July of 1956. There were many and varied trips on freight empty stock and light engine running like the adjoining extract from passed fireman George (Tag) Ashworth's notebook. Just why we were taking No. 90725 to Rose Grove I no longer remember. One thing I do remember was the rough riding of all these locos earned them various nicknames, Bulldozers and Tarboilers were favourites.

Photo: the late B. Hilton.

inside the firebox, plus oil bottle and oil can were all on the footplate. Some of the more zealous "Tool Kings" would scout around the shed for spare fire irons and stand them up in a corner at the top of number five road so he had a pool of them to call on in an emergency. When an engine from a foreign shed was going back to its depot, if it had not arrived with fire irons of doubtful quality, it was certainly going to depart with them, though some of the firemen of a more awkward variety would throw off the poor quality tackle, and would then demand the presence of the "Tool King to put matters right. Good tackle seldom found its way back to its home depot, and Bolton was no different than

continued on page 20

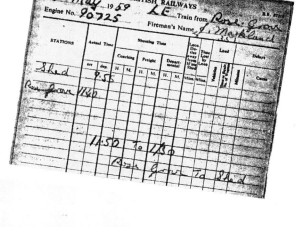

"Lanky" visitor to Bolton Depot

Fresh from overhaul at Horwich, 0-6-0 saddletank No. **51484**, built by Beyer, Peacock in 1882 as a tender engine, was rebuilt in the saddle tank form in 1898. The Aspinall rebuild will work on until June 1959. No shedplate is fitted, the loco eventually making Gorton its home depot after some running in at Bolton. Date of this view is August 25th 1955.

Brian E. Morrison.

anywhere else. Disposal firemen would also be on the lookout for good fire irons,and woe betide any "Tool King"that pinched tackle from the ash pit. Many of the disposal firemen kept their prized posessions hidden in "secret" places ready for the next days work.   Later on in years, as equipment became in short supply, the instruction was that all tackle excepting the fire irons had to be deposited in the stores prior to the engine being stabled. Here, the engine's number would be chalked on the shovel which was then stood in the bucket along with the spanners and other equipment and the two headlamps placed in front on the floor. From there, they were collected by the crew when they signed on for preparation duties. Whilst on the subject of headlamps, one ex LNWR man, Jimmy Jones, referred to them as "Moon Boxes". With their large magnifying bullseye in the front, and the soft somewhat silvery light that they emitted I cannot think of a better name for them. Now that we had become passed cleaners, it was felt by those higher up that we could be entrusted with the post of steamraiser when staff shortages so decreed. As an engine was finished with by the disposal gang, and put into the shed, there would only be a little "live" fire, usually just inside the firebox under the door. The boiler would require filling and, as the engine entered the shed, like as not, the injector would be on. From this point, the steamraiser took over, built up the fire, kept boiler water level topped up and saw to it that there would be sufficient steam pressure for the time when the engine needed to be moved during preparation work, perhaps in a few hours time. Here was a good way of gaining experience in the use of the different types of injectors fitted to each class of engine. Here also was a chance to perfect a technique shown to me by one of the "Old Hand" drivers, double clacking.The LMS standard live steam injectors, particularly as fitted to the Stanier 2-6-4 tanks, were perfect pests to knock of with great waste of water. Most of these injectors would work with the water regulating handle in the middle of its operational span. Such was the use of these injectors, that the water regulating lever was seldom moved from this central position, with the result that they became difficult to

operate through lack of use and lack of proper lubrication. Once the injector had been made to work in the usual manner, the technique was to turn the injector steam valve until it was almost closed. On doing this, a fairly obvious click was heard and water would be seen to issue from the overflow pipe. Quick as a flash, open water regulating valve to full and re open steam valve a couple of turns. Used in this manner, they seldom knocked off and the boiler was filled up much quicker. By far the most difficult shift for the steamraiser was 8.00am Sunday, when about twenty or thirty engines would need lighting up. There were usually two to do this and you did half each. Firstly, every engine would have its firebox "coaled round" with a small space left on the grate inside the door where a couple of lighted firelighters were placed. Once lit, coal was placed around and on top of the firelighters, and from this stage the fire would slowly spread to the rest of the coal in the firebox. When authority decreed it, a wagon of wood off-cuts arrived at the shed for use when lighting up engine fireboxes. The wood was seldom used for this purpose,and as passed cleaners, we were often employed with wheelbarrows, depositing the stuff on any and every available footplate, just to be rid of it. During the winter months there were always the frost fires to be kept going in freezing conditions. Each of the water columns in the shed yard had a brazier placed by it in order to prevent it from freezing up. These and the hose on the ash disposal pit and sump were often kept going by a passed cleaner. In the course of the midnight shift there was always the possibility that a booked fireman would "duck", or fail to turn up. This would then give the senior passed cleaner a firing turn. It was on one such occasion that I experienced my first main line turn,early in 1957, as we shall see in a later chapter.

The unmistakable atmosphere of a working steam shed in the mid 1960s. Taken from in between numbers five and six roads at Bolton shed, both varieties of the Stanier machine are on view along with the inevitable Austerity 2-8-0 in this undated scene.   *P. Salveson.*

From the top of Bolton's coaling plant, in this October 1957 scene, the morning motor is visible beneath on the ash pit. In front of the shed a 2-6-4 tank, 0-8-0, 7F, aWD 2-8-0, another 2-6-4 tank, an 8F 2-8-0, a couple of L&Y 0-6-0s and a 4F. In the immediate background, Beehive Nos.1 and 2 Mills loom ever large, lending yet more atmosphere to the scene. *Colin Boocock.*

A visitor from the White Rose county. Ex L&Y class 3F 0-6-0 No.**52515** carries the larger form of cab numerals as she rests on No.13 road outside Bolton shed. At this time, 1957, the engine's home depot was Low Moor (56F). In March of 1959 it moved to Mirfield (56D), in May 1961 it went back to Low Moor and finally, in February of 1962 its final working home was Sowerby Bridge (56E). Interestingly, No.52515 was the 1st L&Y loco built with the Schmidt superheater way back in 1906 and is credited as the last of this successful class to be withdrawn in December of 1962, before being taken to Horwich Works in January 1963, for scrapping there in May 1963.

Colin Boocock

After a brief sojourn at Agecroft shed, this little 0-6-0 LMS class 2F dock tank arrived at Bolton during the week commencing 18th November, 1963 and made Bolton its home for the next two years where it was used mostly on the branch at Halliwell. Its next, and final place of work was Horwich works from where it was withdrawn. Driver Jim Murphy is at the controls on Bolton shed at the end of 1963. For many years Jim was our union representative on Sectional Council. His dress here is a far cry from smart black trilby and overcoat when on union business.

Colin Boocock

That First Firing Trip - on 49544

Austin Seven, No.**49544**, the engine I will always remember as the loco on my very first firing turn on November 12th 1956. Kearsley pilot was a pleasant shunting turn, but because of the heavy nature of the work,the Austins on that job got rather a thrashing. In this October 1st 1957 view on Bolton shed, No.**49544** still looks quite presentable about two years after her last visit to Horwich for repairs.

Colin Boocock.

Chapter Four

"Get thi traps an' gu wi' Noey, Kearsley pilot".That was the introduction to my first firing turn on Monday November 12th, 1956. The words were uttered by Wilf Bottomley, the telephone attendent, who had stuck his head round the door of the sandhole where I'd been busy about my sand drying activites. The term, "get thi traps", simply meant that I was to collect serge jacket and haversack, together with lunch and brew can from the peg where they hung in the mess room, along with any other items needed.   That Monday morning in 1956, I'd booked on at 7.00am, my first day as a passed cleaner never dreaming that I'd get my first firing turn. It was 9.00am, so I'd make some overtime too.   We were soon on our way walking to Moses Gate to catch a train which would take us to Kearsley where we would relieve the pilot. As we walked by the side of the Down goods loop and passing Beehive Mills, there was a slightly anxious look on Noey's face and it wasn't long before he asked if I could clean a fire. I was able to re-assure him that I'd had plenty of experience in that direction, having helped the disposal gangs frequently. From then onwards, Noey assumed a more relaxed look and we chatted about the news of the day as we walked. Noey, real name Noah Howarth, was one of the old school, white haired, about five feet six inches tall and just over sixty years of age. He always carried his "Tommy Box", containing sandwiches and brew can under his arm. A short train ride and we arrived at Kearsley where we alighted and walked the short distance to the sidings. There, we were to relieve the men on the early turn, the crew having booked on at 2.55am. After preparing three engines, including their own, they had worked a trip from Bullfield Up Sidings, tender first to Kearsley Sidings, having left the shed at 5.25am. As was usual at this period in time, our engine was an "Austin Seven" 0-8-0 of class 7F, and for an Austin was in pretty good order. The crew we were relieving had their traps ready, and after the usual exchange of conversation, started to

make their way back to Bolton shed to sign off duty. Both Noey and I climbed on board, checked boiler water level and the condition of the fire, both were satisfactory, No.**49544** was ready for her days work with us. Kearsley Sidings lay at the side of the main Bolton to Manchester line, and at the foot of the short single mineral line to Linneyshaw Moss, where it linked up with the N.C.B colliery network. The gradient up the branch was fairly steep, about 1 in 50, so quite naturally, loadings were moderate, 16 loaded coal wagons, or, very often 40 empties, quite enough for an Austin. On a wet or greasy rail the loadings could be difficult. In later years,when these locos were badly run down we have often slipped ourselves to a standstill, due to a combination of the latter, wet rails and a load just a little too much for them to move. On these occasions I have nipped off the footplate with the firing shovel, taken sand from the leading sand box and scattered it on the rail to help get a better grip. Unlike some local pilots, actual shunting at Kearsley was minimal and was carried out on a favourable gradient. For a great part of the working day we were engaged on moving loaded coal wagons up the single line to Linneyshaw Moss, from where the N.C.B.'s own locos would take them on to collieries for washing. The vast majority of this traffic was brought to Kearsley by Clifton pilot with Agecroft men on board and was from collieries in the Salford area which had no facilities to wash their own coal. Of course, the old adage of what goes up must come down again was particularly true at Kearsley. The coal that went up the branch for washing had, eventually to come back down again. A train of about forty loaded would be put together at Linneyshaw Moss, with brake van behind. So that the foreman shunter down at Kearsley would know where to set the points for, a code of whistles had been devised and as the train approached the foot of the incline the enginemen would sound the loco whistle. As the train was being pieced together, the shunter would tell the driver how many wagons and would tell him to whistle six leckie or to whistle four. I have to confess that I never fully absorbed this code,but it always seemed to work. After whistling at the foot of the incline, after a short break whilst the points were set, the peg would come off, or we got a green flag from the ground frame. Because the incline was so steep, a good number of wagons had their brakes pinned down in order to prevent a runaway. This would be done as the train was being dragged out of the siding and on to the single line, causing plenty of violent wheelslip. Our first trip, on this my first firing turn was sixteen loaded wagons of power station slack, all of which were for washing. "Oppn thi' damper,an' pur a feyèr on Jim" came the command from Noey. I didn't need a second telling and was keen to get on with it. About six or seven shovels of coal down each side of the firebox, two in each corner under the door,and three or four under the door itself, and just for good measure a couple under the brick arch. We backed on to the brake van, and the shunter who will ride with us, one Harry Bird by name, climbed on board just as I finished putting the fire on, closed the firedoors, and knocked the blower valve off a bit. Sticking my head out of the cab side, the smoke was just rolling off the chimney top so thick you could have sat on it. Just at that point, Noey turned round to reverse the engine, having got the signal from the guard that we were coupled on to the brake van. Seeing the black smoke, Noey wasn't amused at all, he whipped open the firedoors, and applied the blower valve, muttering something about the possibilities of being sacked for making black smoke. I had succeeded in obliterating most of nearby Stoneclough Village and was reminded that the stationmaster lived in one of the adjacent houses, he would be on us like a ton of bricks.   On that Monday morning in late Autumn, although the rail was dry, there was still a good deal of slipping, we always seemed to set off on the curve and we had about 250 tons on our tail. Once on the straight line, we whistled for the level crossing gates to be opened which allowed traffic to cross the line into the nearby factory about a couple of hundred yards away.   Working on just over half regulator,and about 45% cut off, we made steady progress past the level crossing, and underneath the main Manchester to Bolton road. From here it was always much easier on almost straight track, and although the working of the engine was heavy, a couple of rounds of firing of the firebox would generally see you to the top.   On arrival at the top of the incline we stopped clear of all points whilst the shunter alighted with the Annet's key to open the ground frame which would then allow him to operate the points enabling us to continue into the sidings We were now on a right hand curve, so the fireman had to look out for the guards stop signal so he could unhook the brake van and stop it clear of all roads. The rest of the train was then drawn into one of the empty roads, wagon brakes pinned down and the engine detached. It was only on arriving at Linneyshaw Moss that we could find out if there would be any return traffic, there being no telephone system between that point and Kearsley. On this first trip there was no return traffic, so we ran over the points and reversed back down an empty road,tender first to our brake van, where our guard was waiting to couple up to our tender. After reversing the points,and locking up the ground frame,the shunter on such occasions would ride in the brake van which we would propel back to Kearsley.   By the time lunch-time had arrived we had made three trips up the branch and the tender water tank was getting low, the time,about 12.15pm, so we made our way, light engine to the bottom of the yard and carried out loco duties, filling the water tank, cleaning

the fire, getting rid of all the clinker, and with the coal pick, bringing some coal to the front of the tender ready for the rest of the days work. Some time later, after consuming chicken sandwiches and most of a can of tea, Dick Howarth, the foreman shunter wandered down. We could all see that he was getting fidgety, so there were no arguments as he sent us, engine and brake van up the incline to see if there was any return traffic for us on The Moss. Just as we left the yard, Clifton pilot was arriving with another load of power station slack for washing, so when we got back there would be more work for us.   Arriving at Linneyshaw Moss, there were two full roads of wet power station slack, just over forty wagons. Once the frame and the points it controlled were opened, we carried on, engine and brake van to the other end of the sidings. There, the brake van was loose shunted on to one road containing the traffic, the points reversed and we ran back, tender first down the same road which we had just come up. At the opposite end we stopped clear of the points which when reversed, would enable us to couple up to one line of vehicles, draw them out again, clear of the points enabling us to propel them on to the other wagons with the brake van behind them. Our train was now ready for departure and in the manner previously described, we dragged the train out of the sidings, slipping violently many times because of the weight, and the number of brakes being "pinned " down to assist the engine's brake on the incline. There was that strange smell of metal to metal friction,as the tortured engine driving wheels did battle with the shining rail in their struggle for adhesion. As I opened the firebox doors I could observe the reaction of the fire to this rough treatment, amidst the incandescant glow, I could see huge lumps of it dancing up and down in the grate and holes being ripped in the firebed.   Eventually,we got the train on to falling gradient, the regulator was almost shut as we kept a sharp lookout for the signal from the guard on the brake van so that we knew that the shunter had re-set the catch points, locked up the ground frame and re-joined the train. From here on we should, if the ground staff have put sufficient brakes down, hold them with comparative ease with the engine's steam brake. Occasionally, applying the tender hand brake would almost be sufficient, thus saving continually applying and releasing the steam brake which, on these Austins was not of the graduable variety.   When the tender brake was applied,and when the engine's steam brake was not, a sort of shuttling motion was set up twixt engine and tender, causing the intermediate buffing gear to come in to contact with a loud thump, each revolution of the driving wheels. On this trip down the incline,once we had whistled six leckie,just as we were coming to a stand, we got the signal to proceed, and gradually, with the weight on our tail, we released our engine's brake, and getting them on to the stretch, quickly picking up speed in order to drag them clear into the siding around the right hand curve we jolt over the points. On some occasions we have slipped ourselves to a standstill before dragging them clear, even though some of the train was still on a falling gradient. Here, I'd hop off with the brakestick and lift up some of the wagon brakes until we could shift them again.   That afternoon we made another two trips up the incline with "washers"to Linneyshaw Moss, returning on each occasion engine and brake van, and on the second return trip our relief was awaiting us at the level crossing gates on our way down. Once we had arrived back in the sidings our relief took over.

"Austin Seven's" at Bolton

Whilst working with passed fireman Jack Swarbrick during January 1959, on engine No.**49662**, on a Horwich to Ashton Moss freight we suffered a hot big end whilst climbing the bank out of Manchester Victoria to Miles Platting. This caused the metal to run, and as a consequence, No.**49662** was sidelined, never to work again. The loco stood on Bolton's scrap road on the Crescent Road side of the shed for about eighteen months, before being moved in October 1961 to Central Wagon Co. Ince, Wigan. 49662 did not finally disappear until April of 1962. I often wonder how much longer she would have survived without this incident. Date of this photograph, September 17th 1960.

Roy Panting

The remains of tea in our brewcans were emptied on to the coal in the tender, belongings gathered up and our relief assured that the fire had been cleaned. We alighted from the footplate of No.**49544** and made our way the short distance to Kearsley station where we would catch the 3.32pm stopper from Manchester Vic. This first firing turn had been a success, the engine had steamed well all day, next time I fired for Noey he'd remember my competence. I pondered how long it would be before I got my next firing turn; one thing was for sure, now I'd had my appetite whetted, I'd be ready for it.

During the latter half of 1957, December to be precise, there arrived at Bolton a couple of "Austin 7s" as replacements for other members of the class which had been withdrawn. Nos.**49618** & **49662** arrived from Lees (Oldham) depot and straightaway both gained a reputation as the most run down and roughest riding locos at Bolton, and we'd swapped two reasonable Austerities for them - some swap! Imagine our surprise though, as passed cleaners, when one of our number returning from a visit to Horwich for spares reported that 49618 was being given a General overhaul, and that he had seen the loco stripped right down to the frames. What a difference it was weeks later, to ride on the footplate of an Austin Seven that did not feel as if it was trying to shake itself to pieces. The 0-8-0 is seen at Kearsley sidings during the summer of 1958 on the middle shift of the pilot there.

Author.

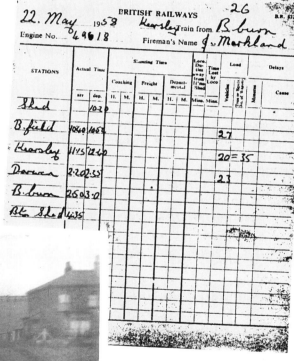

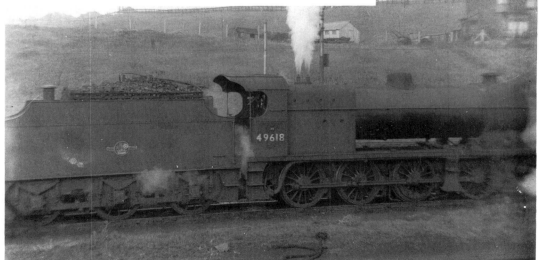

Firing in the old man's link

Chapter Five

As a passed cleaner, the work one did was as varied as were the signing on times and the drivers you worked with. Logically, one might assume that as a driver got older and more experienced, he might get a little more tolerent. Sadly, this was not always the case, some seemed to get more windy as they aged. There existed at Bolton, two old mens' links, one known as Kearsley Pilot Link with ten sets of men, and the other known as the Yard Pilot Link with six sets of men. The firemen that were marked in these links were the senior passed firemen,and, especially in the latter link, seldom actually worked with the driver with whom they were paired, they themselves would be carrying out driving duties, covering for men off sick or perhaps annual leave. Of these two local links, the yard pilot link carried the more restricted route availability because the drivers placed in it would be there owing to either a medical or eyesight problem. Kearsley Pilot Link with its ten sets of men encapsulated drivers who felt that they were not suited to the rigours of the more demanding main line work. So on attaining the age of sixty years, they could, when a vacancy arose in the link,apply to come off main line work and take their final years in a more leisurely manner. Now I suppose everyone has their own pet "hate", some drivers literally hated oiling the engines they worked with and would use every excuse for not so doing. Firemen hated having to get on the tank top to fill up with water or having to clean the fire, especially when they felt it was not necessary to do so, and that in their view was most times. As a very raw recruit, and still with a great deal to learn, especially about drivers and their dislikes I signed on one Sunday morning at 6.00am in the early Summer of 1957 to work a ballast train in Bolton station. The driver was from Kearsley Pilot Link, Ernie Rothwell, a man for whom the rule book didn't seem to exist, he was always willing to make the job as easy as possible. Although I didn't know it,at that time,Ernie's pet hate was oiling engines, I was soon to find out. Power for this easy day's work was an ex L&Y "A" Class 3F number **52348**. That Sunday morning, I'd arrived well before Ernie,

drawn all the tackle from the stores and left the oil to warm for him on the hob over the firedoors, that would make it easier for him to use so I thought. Some ten or fifteen minutes later Ernie arrived on the scene complete with dish wrapped in newspaper containing egg and bacon ready for frying on the shovel once we'd got settled in Bolton station. Thinking I'd done him a favour by putting the oil to warm, I told him where I had left it. "Chuck it in the bloody firebox", he barked without so much as stopping to bid me good morning, continuing as he did to the office to sign on duty. I was flabbergasted but could see he meant it. For the next few minutes I busied myself with the usual preparation duties, the longest of which always seemed to be the filling of the cylinder lubricator with the thick, treacle-like substance which we had nicknamed "Bovril". Ernie arrived back on the scene just as I was throwing the bag out of the tender tank and could see I was somewhat exasperated by his outburst. His philosophy was simple, in all probability we would be doing less work with our engine than the shed shunt, and they certainly didn't bother to oil their engine. There was no need either for us to oil our engine. In the end he was proved correct, once we had got our train in position by about 7.30am, we never moved again during our shift, just after 12.00 noon our relief arrived. Unfortunately,Ernie's relief did not share the same convictions and was of the opposite point of view. Harold Bailey was one of the old school, who, to us passed cleaners was someone to be avoided at all costs. He seemed to carry a perpetual chip on his shoulder, seldom approved of anything and if he smiled it was certainly only once every Preston Guild. Harold's first question knowing of Ernie's reputation was a foregone conclusion. "Ha'st eilt it" ? he asked. And of course he got the same response that I had received earlier in the day. As we walked away from **52348** along platform four, on our way back to sign off duty, I cast a glance over my shoulder to see Harold's face, as long as next week, oil can in hand preparing to oil the valve-gear. Although

continued on page 28

Halliwell pilots

← *(Opposite - page 26)* From time to time, there arose at Halliwell a shortage of brake vans to work trains starting there. Not every train arriving at the location terminated there, and although Springs Branch men, working into Halliwell from Bamfurlong, had no return work, they generally took their two brake vans back to the Wigan area with them. Thus, there would be seen in the enginemens arrangements book a note by the side of the driver and fireman, when starting from Halliwell, "Pick up brake van at Burnden". On one such occasion, a Black Five and brake van are pictured running on to the branch at Astley Bridge Junction. *P. Salveson.*

The last day of steam at Halliwell with BR Standard class 2-6-0 No.**78013** providing the power. *P.Salveson.*

A BR Standard class 2MT 2-6-0 No.**78055** takes a breather outside the cabin at Halliwell. Only toward the end of the 1950s was it thought necessary to provide a water supply. Formerly, water had to be carried, usually on the footplate, from the goods office further down the yard *P.Salveson.*

Orlando Bridge, or simply "OB" was the signing on point for goods guards and was often the place where relief of either guard or locomen took place. The small brick building to right of camera contained the nerve centre complete with class one goods inspector. The siding immediately in front of the building was always known as two old, and trains such as the early evening Blackburn to Ancoats fitted freight would pick up traffic from there. On the left is the goods warehouse where vans were loaded. The scene is bathed in afternoon sunshine as Bolton Black Five No.**45104** performs station pilot duties. *Bart van der Leeuw.*

continued from page 26

Ernie had come off main line work in order to take light work, no one could ever accuse him of being windy. Quite the opposite, he was always ready for a laugh, and that pipe of his with its thick twist, combined with the effects of the sulphur tablets that he took had on the atmosphere in the immediate vicinity had to experienced to be believed. Ernie was the sort of person you always wanted to be marked with, the reason being, that for most of the days work you did most of the driving, and the firing too of course. A firm favourite for this sort of work was Halliwell pilot. We would book on at 5.28am and leave the shed at 5.43am,the engine having been prepared by turn 221F, one of three locos prepared by the men on the early turn of Kearsley pilot. At this period in time, 1957, the engine was under normal circumstances an ex L&Y saddletank. For the first part of the working, Ernie would be at the regulator, and en route to Bullfield, light engine, we would stop at Orlando Bridge, the guards signing on point to pick up our guard, continuing on from there to Bullfield Up Sidings, right next to where the gasworks once stood. There were still quite a number of coal merchants using the yard at Halliwell, the goods warehouse was still quite busy, and Charles Turner, paper makers, also had a warehouse where pulp was delivered , sometimes in very large amounts. Add to the foregoing, the power station traffic and the vast numbers of condemned wagons or "Internal Use" only stock which were moved to Halliwell in store, it can be seen that on some occasions there could be a heavy train waiting for this early morning trip.These little saddletanks of L&Y vintage were quite strong, but about 14 of coal was more than enough for them to drag on to the branch via Astley Bridge junction, anything more and banking assistance was taken from Bradshawgate. Departure time was set at 6.20am, and if we had a full load on we would make our way very carefully, through the tunnels beneath Moor Lane, keeping the train in check in order to avoid a runaway. With anything under,or approching a full load we would have a dash at them, first of all requesting that the distant in the tunnels be lowered, giving us a clear run through Bradshawgates section. No sooner had we stopped at Halliwell than Ernie would pick up his newspaper and take his brewcan and dish with the usual fry up in it to the cabin, that was the last you saw of him until it was time to leave to shunt the NCB sidings at Bradshawgate en route to shed for loco duties and relief at lunchtime, six hours home rule driving and firing. The shunters cabin at Halliwell was fairly spacious but also very basic. Arriving there at about 6.35am,the first job was to find the key to unlock the door. The next priority was to light the fire in the stove, fill the kettle and get it on to boil. In my early railway days, there wasn't even a water supply to the cabin, this had to be fetched in large emamelled cans from the office adjacent to the goods warehouse. By the time we had shunted our train, there was a good chance the stove would be hot enough to cook on, and that the water in the kettle would be almost on the boil, ready to brew a can or two of tea. Halliwell was not directly connected to a control circuit telephone, the latter" nerve centre" had to be contacted via Astley Bridge junction signalbox. Halliwells telephone was of the antiquated variety having separate ear and mouthpiece, the earpiece hung on its hook at the side of the 'phone and the mouthpiece screwed on at the front of the box, serving, most days, as an impromptu egg cup for the yard foreman's staple diet. With the breakfast formalities out of the way there was plenty of shunting to do, the private traders sidings to be serviced, loaded wagons in and empty ones taken out, and both "New" and "Old" leckies to be shunted. At this late stage, 1957,

it was strange for young ears to hear the electricity works referred to as the "L.E.P.",Lancashire Electric Power. On certain days it was a bonus to travel down "the branch" to Astley Bridge yard, the end of the line, along which, passenger trains once travelled. Although these had ceased in 1879, the terminus becoming a coal yard only, terms such as, platform road, and main line still persisted, though entry into some of the sidings was on a "wing and a prayer" basis, such was the state of the metals. With the first part of this job there were many occasions when, leavingBullfield with just under a full load we had got the distant in the tunnels and had a dash at them. Alas, on some mornings if the rail was damp you started to slip after Craddock Lane just as you felt the full weight of the train behind you, and if the sanders weren't working well, then inevitably the sheer weight would drag you to a stand. On some occasions we've been going so slowly because of adverse conditions that it was possible to pile some sand on the firing shovel from the box located beneath the floorboards, nip off the footplate, and sand the rail ahead of the engine, thus preventing stalling on the main line and possibly causing delay to the following 6.55am pasenger out of Bolton. As previously noted, these little saddle tanks were pretty strong for their size,but one morning on this same job, there was a right raft of 27 loaded coal wagons waiting for us and **51498** when we backed up in Bullfield Up Sidings, most of which were 16 tonners. Considering that these little engines weighed under 44 tons, and, if each of those 16 ton wagons were full, the train weight was something like 400 tons, it exceeded the engine's weight by about ten times. On this occasion I was firing for a man named Bill("Flogger") Hogget, and knowing of his reputation I'd put a fire on to suit, just in case. It was as well I had done so, in view of what was awaiting us. Leaving Bullfield Up Sidings,we made our way extra carefully towards Bolton West's section having requested that we should have a clear run through that and Bradshawgate's section because of the heavy load. Eventually, as we crept through the darkness of the tunnel beneath Moor Lane and Newport Street we sighted the signals, both home and distant of the lower quadrant variety at clear. Bill made a determined effort, first of all, gently taking up the slack between all the loose coupled wagons and opened up **51498**. With the flanges of the driving wheels screaming their protest at this sort of treatment over the sharply curved Johnson Street connecting line, and much tugging and pulling as the couplings tightened we flailed past the clear distant signal for Bradshawgate and plunged into the tunnel beneath the latter road with the regulator right over in its quadrant block and the engine's exhaust doing its best to blast away the tunnel lining. As we roared past the siding where the bank engine stood, I caught a glimpse of the crew on the "Crab" 2-6-0 as they warmed their loco up in readiness to bank us, they were open mouthed as we powered our way on, toward the switched-out Craddock Lane signal box, beyond which we would stop for the banker to come behind us. There, to this day I remember Bill actually applying the vacuum brake well before we came to a stand, even though we were now on a rising gradient. Just before coming to a stand, Bill, obviously as excited as I was, shouted across the footplate, over the screaming din of the safety valves blowing off that we could have "swung" them on to the branch without the assistance of the banker. Whilst I have to admit that whilst we were going along great guns at one stage, it did seem just possible, but,realistically, on that sharp left hand curve at Astley Bridge junction, and a steep gradient, we would have, inevitably been dragged to a stand. When we remember that these little class 2F engines were re builds of a design introduced as long ago as 1877 and were still giving good service as late, certainly as 1961, the soundness of their construction was undoubted. For the sort of work expected of them, they were really useful engines. They were easy to operate and during loose shunting operations were in their element. When loose shunting bunker first, it was easy to close the regulator and operate the brake lever with one movement of the left arm. Here, they scored heavily over the 0-6-0 diesels which were eventually to replace them. They could also be reversed whilst still on the move, something else you couldn't do with the diesels. With only seven full turns of the easy to operate reversing wheel from backward to forward gear and vice versa, they could get through their work very quickly. They did however have some shortcomings, one of which was the injectors which just would not work when the water in the saddle tank got low, and as a consequence heated up. On many occasions we had to beat a hasty retreat to the water column, put the hose in the tank and as soon as possible put the injector on to get water level up quickly in the boiler. Without doubt, the busiest shunt job at Bolton was Rose Hill pilot, or as it was better known, number 1 pilot. Until the arrival of the 0-6-0 diesels this turn was the preserve of an 0-6-0 saddletank of L&Y vintage with automatic vacuum brake, this latter being needed in order to test the vacuum brake on loaded vans from the warehouse as they were made up into trains. Rose Hill sidings were far from well suited to loose shunting operations. We would drop down light engine into the yard and drag out a raft of wagons for sorting out, uphill until just about on the bridge which crossed Manchester Road. From that point, the gradient fell toward the shunting neck and eventually, the buffers, or if we had to drag out a particularly long rake of wagons, out main line. Occasionally, with a heavy load and a wet rail I have wondered if we would stop in time before running into the buffers, on several shunts we have been on the slide, wheels locked, before coming safely to a stand. Depending on the length of train that we had dragged out of the yard, three-quarters of the vehicles could be on a falling gradient when the shunter stopped us. The engine was then reversed and, consequently, you were then loose shunting on an adverse gradient with most of the train. Three or four shunts only and then the operation was repeated until all the vehicles had been disposed of into their respective roads. One evening in 1957 I was firing on the 5.25pm turn of Rose Hill pilot. The night turn, 10.00pm ground staff came on duty and made a prompt start, and in the manner previously described, we shunted the yard, none stop, with trips down toward the warehouse until ten minutes past one (am) when a well earned brew was taken, such was the amount of traffic handled at that time, our relief arriving minutes later. It was on number one pilot that I nearly gave one old hand driver a heart attack. Bill Read was a quiet sort of chap, you could almost describe him as an old dear, and unlike some of the other drivers in the link, seemed quite content with his work. Bill and I had been working the 12.50am turn at RoseHill with ex L&Y saddletank number **51408**, we had had a fairly busy shift. The time had reached about 5.20am and we had finished work, so far as the 10.00pm ground staff were concerned. At this time of day it was customary to clean the fire, and on these little engines there was a neat arrangement. A small rectangular section of the grate, about a foot square could be lifted up with the short "Lanky" pricker and then placed on one side in the grate. Any ash or clinker could then be pushed through into the ash pan via the hole in the grate, after which, the section was then replaced. The clinker and ash were then raked out of the ashpan with a suitably shaped bar which resided permanently in the

sidings for just that purpose, ten minutes and the job was done. Our coal bunker that day contained a mixture of best Yorkshire steam coal, slabs of it, combined with a sprinkling of ovoids, coal eggs, it produced little in the way of ash or clinker. Looking into the firebox, all that could be seen was a very fine coating of grey dust, the fire was very low. My sentiments were that the fire didn't need touching. Bill, drawing thoughtfully on his pipe opined otherwise, suggesting that I knock a bit out, so that, of course, we could then say quite truthfully, to our relief that the fire had indeed been cleaned. Unfortunately, I was over zealous, so thin was the fire that I succeeded in knocking most of it through into the ashpan. Panic was written all over Bill's face as I started to coal around and on top of what was left of the fire, Bill saying that it would never get going again in t' memory 'o' mon. I could almost hear his heartbeat speed up as he assured me he would never trust me with anything again. Luckily, the Austerity waiting to work Rose Hill-Bury was still standing in the nearby cattle dock and Albert Higson, it's fireman, was only too willing to oblige with some "live" fire. Several shovels of live fire were carried to our "dying" engine and more piled around and on top of it. Within minutes we would be back to normal and so too Bill's blood pressure. A few weeks later I succeeded in raising it again, almost losing the shovel on Bullfield pilot this time on an ex L&Y "A" Class number **52350**. How I managed to leave go of that shovel I'll never know, but one look at Bill's face was enough to tell me he'd not forgotten the episode of only weeks earlier. The day shift of Bullfield pilot, turn number 290F was a fairly cosy affair even though as late as August 1962, Bolton still managed to turn out an ex L&Y "A" Class in the shape of **52345** which had been around at Bolton at least since August of 1959, and was still, externally at any rate, in a most respectable condition after its 1958 General overhaul at Horwich. Leaving the shed at 9.25am, tender first to Bullfield, light engine, some time would be spent shunting the Down side. Signals for these operations from the shunter or guard were always on the firemans side, so it was necessary to put a good fire on, so that it would last a good while, in order that the fireman could devote his time to watching for and relaying the signals to the driver. A lot of coal traffic was handled at Bullfield, some for the gas works, some for the many coal yards in and around Bolton, and of course, power station slack for both Kearsley and Halliwell power stations. A short shunting neck was provided on the Up side terminating in buffers, short of the tunnel wall. Occasionally however, because wagons at the far end of a siding had to be moved it was necessary to draw out on to the main line. This meant very often, that you were shunting in the tunnel, and, once again on an unfavourable gradient. What with fumes in the tunnel, and nineteen turns of the reversing wheel from full forward to full back gear, it could, needless to say, be a tiresome operation. In the late afternoon, once the train had been pieced together, at about 5.00pm our last job on this turn was to work the trip into Burnden sidings, here, we were booked to be relieved at 5.26pm. Our relief from Kearsley Pilot Link had signed on at 5.6pm for their turn 291F. After the prescribed ten minutes for notice reading they would make their way the short walk to Burnden Sidings to await arrival of the Bullfield trip which now formed Burnden pilot, or as it was better known, number 3 pilot. It was this latter job, one evening very early in 1957 that formed my second firing turn, and again it was an "A" Class, this time No.**52389**. Number three pilot never ventured far, it's outer limits being the warehouse by the side of Manchester Road, to collect the fitted vans for the evening Brindle Heath to Carlisle freight which called at Burnden to pick up. Usually, this short journey involved the pilot travelling "facing road" along the Up goods line round the back of East cabin, and back again over the same metals, this time of course right road with the vans to Burnden where they were shunted into their appropriate roads. Not many trains actually started out of the Burnden end of the sidings, they merely called to pick up or set down traffic, in a few cases they terminated there as did Goole to Burnden or Calder Bridge to Burnden, those calling in were the Brindle Heath job, Bury Deal Street, various Bamfurlong jobs and of course there were the many trip and shunt jobs such as Moses Gate pilot. In later years after the closure of Bury MPD, there was an early morning trip to Bury, the loco going on from the latter to form Castleton Pilot. In later years on withdrawal of the trains from Brindle Heath, the retimed 8.45pm Ancoates to Carlisle called in to pick up this

continued on page 31

Moses Gate and Halliwell pilots

Ex L&Y saddle tank No.**51486** brings the 1/00pm trip from Moses Gate to Burnden on completion of its stint as the morning pilot there. The train is pictured passing under Burnden junctions signal gantry on to the fork line in June 1960. Formerly L&Y number 585 of 1881, the loco was withdrawn two months after this photo was taken.
J.Houghton.

The 0-6-0 class 3F tank engines of Midland parentage were far from a common sight in the Bolton area, still less those fitted with condensing apparatus, though Bolton did have some members of the class in later years. A local freight trip from Haslams sidings to Halliwell or possibly Bullfield on an unknown date is operated by No.**47217** passing Bolton East Junction. *J.Houghton.*

traffic. The trains that did start from these sidings actually did so from the opposite end which was known as "Haslams" sidings (the Bury trip excepted) two of which were 11.22pm Bolton to Blackpool and the 11.40pm Bolton to Colne. Of course, there were other trains starting from Haslams, but in most cases their destinations were of a local nature only, most of them ending up at Horwich, the loco works being in full swing. On this second firing turn, I was making my way back to the footplate of **52389** when I spotted something on the ground by the side of a wagon which I thought was wheat. As I bent down, under the soft and somewhat inadequate light emitted from the lamps in the sidings, I noticed that it, or rather they, were moving. Without picking it up, closer examination revealed that it or rather they were in fact white maggots, then I noticed the smell coming from the wagon above them and read its label. It was in fact a wagon of bones for the glue factory at Appley Bridge on the line to Southport, the thing must have been teeming with the insects. It was always difficult to make a full day out of this job, and sometimes well nigh impossible. Often, by the time midnight arrived the goods department had finished with us, there was, quite simply, no more work for us, so we were sent to the shed. We were just over an hour short of a day and so ended up disposing of the engine, for which we were allowed 45 minutes for anything less than a class 5 engine. One job which, at the time of which I write, the late fifties, could be relied upon to produce a varied diet of motive power was the afternoon Moses Gate Pilot. Signing on at 11.25am there was a short walk to Bolton station to relieve Wigan L&Y men who had worked into Bolton with one of their own engines. The power could be an ex LMS superheater 2P 4-4-0, either **40587** or **40680**, often it was a Derby Four, **44220**, **44221** or **44225**. Coming a little more modern it could be any of Wigan's Stanier or Fairburn 2-6-4 tanks. For us though, at that time, the ultimate was a B.R. Standard class 2MT, 2-6-0, either of **78061/2/3/4**. Because of the operation of the reversing wheel on the latter 2-6-0's we nicknamed them "bacon slicers". After running light engine to the shed, the fire was cleaned, the water tank and coal space topped up. Next, the engine would be backed up to the train which had been made up on the shed loop by the 7.30am disposal gang. This would consist of coal empties, wagons of ash from the ash pit and occasionally a wagon or two containing heavy locomotive parts for Horwich Works. This little train of about ten or twelve wagons with tail lamp hung on the hook of the last vehicle, and the guard riding on the footplate, would make its way up the shed yard, out via the main line, on to the fork at Burnden, where, once clear of all points, brakes would be pinned down, the engine detached, and then run round the train. There, shunting took place in the sidings and another formation would be made up consisting of wagons for repair at the Central Wagon Works on the opposite side of the main line to Bolton shed, and empties for the scrap dock on the Up side at Moses Gate. On arrival at the Central Wagon Works, newly repaired wagons were shunted out, and other wagons left there for repairs. At Moses Gate, once again the engine ran round its train to enable the scrap dock to be shunted, loaded ones out, empty ones in. Next, the whole of what was left was taken over to the Down side. There, more shunting took place and, more importantly, traffic out of the warehouse. At that time, Moses Gate warehouse and goods yard were still quite busy and in addition, there was a road motor depot where driver and vehicle training was undertaken. Alas, all of the foregoing has now disappeared. Around teatime, about 5.00pm in fact, a train of about twenty vehicles having

been made up, these would be worked up the goods line to Rose Hill sidings. More often than not, we would be kept waiting just by the shed outlet where, most conveniently, there was a water column of the "parachute" variety, there, we could fill up our water tank whilst we waited a path to cross the main line in between the many passenger trains. As soon as there was a suitable break in the mainline activity we crossed over at Burnden junction on to the fork line, just as Lostock Hall men were propelling their nine empty non-corridor coaches over the other line to Moses via the goods line, having worked into Bolton with the 4.57pm from the R.O.F. at Euxton. The end of the day came for Moses Gate pilot on completion of shunting at Rose Hill sidings. From the latter, we ran light engine to the shed, once again over the fork line via Burnden Junction. Arriving on the shed, the engine was left for Wigan L&Y men to collect to be worked back to its home depot on Wigan Parcels.

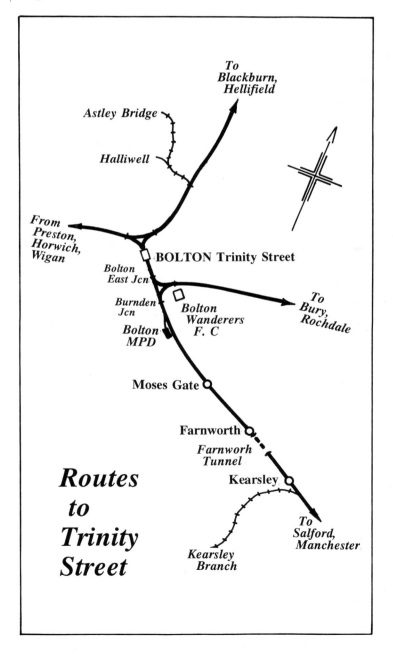

Routes to Trinity Street

Firing Turn No.4
- 40072 to Rochdale and back.

In spotless lined black, Stanier Class 3 passenger tank No.**40072** performs station pilot duties at Blackpool's Central station on 26th May 1959. The locomotive still carries the original form of domeless taper boiler and was the loco which figured in my first main line passenger turn in March 1957.　　　*F. Dean.*

Chapter Six

Bolton shed, 26C, and in later years, 9K, was never famous for it's passenger work. There were regular turns to Blackpool, Liverpool, Southport, Hellifield, Skipton and Todmorden with a late Sunday turn to Wakefield. These were just about the furthest points one could expect to get on passenger work. It was to be expected that a more menial, local trip would be the order of the day for a first passenger turn, and thats just how it was. As mentioned in a previous chapter, it sometimes happened that a fireman, or a senior passed cleaner might "duck", so giving a firing turn to the next most senior passed cleaner not currently marked for firing. Again, thats just how it was. I didn't know it at the time of course, when I signed on for duty at 4.00am one Saturday morning early in 1957, but the passed cleaner marked for the 5.15am stopping train from Bolton to Rochdale had failed to turn in. At the last minute, just before the engine was due off the shed, the running shift foreman, Arthur Hulton, nicknamed "Flashbulb" because of his somewhat eratic manner, came into the cabin telling me to get over to "Raif" Ainscough on **40072** on number seven road straightaway, panic was written all over his face. Ralph had done most of the preparation work on this and two other engines, all I had to do was put the bag in at the water column in order to fill the tanks and just check that there was enough paraffin in the headlamp systers to take us to Rochdale and back. By the time I'd done all that it was almost 4.30am, the time

booked for departure from the shed for this turn, so as soon as we had filled up the water tanks, the fire was spread and it was time to go, bunker first up the shed yard, with mud taps blowing to the ringing out telephone. Three short rings on the press key put me in touch with the signalman at Burnden Junction box. "40072 light engine to Byng Street for 5.15 Rochdale" I said to the train-booker, and he acknowledged my message. I climbed back on to the footplate where Ralph had had just enough time to swill round with the hose pipe. The damp atmosphere on the footplate from the swilling down operation cleared quickly, most of the steam being sucked into the firebox through the open fire-doors. With just below 150lbs. pressure on the gauge there was plenty of steam to take us on our way to the carriage sidings at Byng Street with damper open a little. Seconds later, off came the signal at the shed outlet, it was the lower one of the two, so we were going out main line. We set off, mud taps still blowing in order to allow any water still in the cylinders to be blown away, but as we pass under Burnden Junction's signal gantry, the operating lever was kicked shut by Ralph, just as the distant signal above goes to clear, lending an air of importance to the proceedings. As we moved on rapidly, through the darkness in the crisp Winter air, the only sound to be heard was the barely audible, almost hollow sort of exhaust from **40072's** chimney. Travelling bunker first, visibility was particularly good on these machines as we picked our way through the darkness and under the bright gleaming eyes of East Junction's gantry. As we approached the station, the regulator was closed and the engine allowed to coast along, then, under less favourable signals, we run at reduced speed into the even greater darkness of the tunnel under Newport Street, and in stark contrast to the brightness of the signal gantries, we came to a stand behind the ground signal, clear of the points that would allow us to cross to the up side. These points, controlled from Bolton West box were operated electro-pneumatically, as they went over, we could hear that characteristic tsssssssshhhhhhhhh ock. So we crossed over to the up side beneath the now disappeared girder bridge into number 1 platform, behind another ground signal and, after more point movements, reverse into Byng Street carriage sidings, there,three non-corridor coaches awaited us. Now anyone who has gone through the "hooking on" process will know that when you got the same arrangement of vacuum pipe on the coach as you had on the engine, they were devils to couple up. Because both engine and coach pipes were hanging vertically it was difficult to get the ends of each of them together, and so engage the lugs and fit the pins into position. Here was a situation where practice would make perfect,and the development of strong arm muscles would be an added bonus. Giving me a helping hand, Ralph was somewhat surprised to learn that the loco inspector had offered no guidence relating to coupling up to passenger trains. Once the shackle was on, the two of us together managed to couple the vacuum pipes, Ralph, back on the footplate allowed the engine to ease off the buffers, giving more room to fit the steam heating pipes together. Now, with both of us back on board, we could test the vacuum in the brake system. After opening the steam valve to allow steam to the train heating system we were ready to draw our train into number one platform. The ground signal was off, but we still awaited the arrival of the shunter. "Nip into the first brake van and take the handbrake off" said Ralph. Obediently, I did as he asked, we shuffled quietly out of the siding and ran gently into number 1 platform where the shunter, who had obviously just woken up,awaited us. With about 25 minutes to go to departure time, I was able to get my bearings and prepare for this short journey over the now lifted branch via Bury and Castleton to Rochdale. Looking at the fire, there were some holes in it which I filled up. I then built the fire right up under the door with the dampers now closed, the injector was used to keep the safety valves quiet. Our engine, 40072 of Blackpool, had recently been given an overhaul at Horwich and was well into its trial period. Somehow these class 3 Stanier passenger tanks of 2-6-2 wheel arrangement had been nicknamed "Breadvans", possibly on account of their small,box-like size. Much of the floor boarding had been renewed, new tip up seats for driver and fireman had been supplied. Steam and vacuum gauges were new as was the hose pipe, more regularly known as "the degger", and in the air there was that "new paint" smell. In some books that I've read, the footplates of these machines were described as neat and compact, they were also small. You only needed to have a bunker full of coal eggs on board, and half of it around your ankles to appreciate that fact. Skinned knuckles were also easy to obtain on these footplates when firing. This engine, one of the earlier members of the class, still retained the original variety of domeless boiler. Another original feature retained on the footplate, and not exactly beloved of firemen was "Stanier's ground-frame". This description referred to the levers which operated the dampers and really did look like a small ground-frame. They were neatly placed in just the right spot on the floor, close by the fireman's seat on his left as he faced the front. When the fireman got up from his seat, there was a more than even chance that the bottoms of his overalls would get caught on top of one of the levers with obvious results. By now, the

hands of the large platform clock had crept round to 5.10am, and the guard came up to tell us the train details. With the blower on about a quarter of a turn, and the damper open, the fire was licking its hungry lips that vivid golden red colour in the mouth of the firebox. With a couple of minutes to go, the safety valve lifts, disturbing the peace of the early morning, the steam pressure gauge showing exactly 200lbs per square inch. Silence is restored once the live steam injector is coaxed into its reassuring song, and simultaneously, from the other end of the train, the guard gives the "rightaway" with his green light. We crept,almost stealthily, out of the platform on the beginning of our journey, off went the feed. Between here and East Junction, another round of firing, mainly to the sides and under the door of the firebox as we thread our way through East Junction's"nineties" crossing out on to the main line and into Rose Hill Junction's section. Now,on a falling gradient we quickly picked up speed clattering over the viaducts of Burnden and Darcy Lever and onwards into the darkness beyond, charging at the short sharp climb to Bradley Fold. On this first passenger turn, one of the most difficult things was keeping my feet as we swayed and bounced along. This was something that would come with practice as would firing techniques. With a featherweight load like ours, there was no difficulty maintaining steam pressure, but those small driving wheels of only five feet three inches in diameter seemed totally inadequate for any turn of speed. "There'll be a cup of tea for us when we get to Heywood", said Ralph. I wondered how on earth he knew that. Some time later on in years, I found out that this particular porter who would be on duty when we arrived at Heywood, always made the crew of this train a cup of tea, in exchange for a barrow of coal, when needed, for the waiting room and porters room fires. When we actually arrived at Heywood, true to form, the porter brought us a cup of tea in the usual BTC issue cups, and very welcolme it was, three quarters of the way through our journey. Ten or so minutes later we were arriving at our destination, Rochdale, and once we had come to a stand, the first job was to lower the front headlamp from its position, high up on the smokebox door to a red one in the middle of the front buffer beam. From here we propelled the train out of the station, and into the carriage sidings. There, we uncoupled from our train and placed a white lamp on the middle bracket at the bunker end. At that time, Rochdale possessed a hand operated turntable, but today, we scorned its use as we instead, return to Bolton shed, light engine, via the fork line at Castleton, enabling us to turn on the triangle there and run engine first. Back at the shed there was no escaping disposal duties, we were well short of a day. After throwing out the fire on the ash pit and having stabled 40072 on number 2 road we were kept hanging about until our day was up, about 11.00am for Ralph and noon for me. The end was something of an anti-climax, though there was some consolation for me, extra cash to draw next week and another firing turn under my belt, number 4 out of a required 287 turns which would give me a better rate of pay.

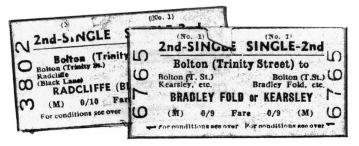

Yorkshire Coal for Liverpool
(First Mainline Freight Turn)

Chapter Seven

During the mid nineteen fifties there were still a number of goods jobs coming out of the Yorkshire area and passing through Bolton. Many of them would be bound for the docks at Liverpool, perhaps carrying coal traffic. Others would arrive at the various sorting sidings in and around the Liverpool area. There were times when late running of these jobs took place, and the men working the train into Lancashire would "wire" for relief, either at Rochdale or Bolton. This would then create a driving turn for the senior passed fireman and a couple of firing turns for passed cleaners. The second most senior passed cleaner would relieve the most senior passed fireman on one of the local shunt turns, whilst the most senior passed cleaner would team up with the passed fireman to relieve the main line goods working. Because the men working out of Yorkshire had been relieved, this meant that they would be unable to take up any booked return workings, so one could have a reasonable days work on such occasions. At this particular time some of the traffic routed via Bolton was, Royston to Garston, Carlton to Garston, Crofton to Fazakerley, Crofton to Edge Hill with locomotive coal for that depot, and Mytholmroyd to Fazakerley. It was to be Carlton to Garston which would give me my first main line goods turn, and in fact, my first real main line job. Signing on one morning in March 1957 at 7.00am, with no prospect of a firing turn, I'd been hanging around until the day foreman cleaner arrived at 8.00am. The 7.30am shed shunt had put a wagon of wet sand outside the sandhole on the shed loop ready for emptying, I was told to make a start on doing just that. By 11.00am I was well into half completing the job, when Tommy Moore, a senior passed fireman came down to the sandhole to ask if I could manage a bit of a main line job. Two minutes later, we were on our way, walking to Bolton station to relieve Carlton to Garston, a coal train out of the Yorkshire coal fields. Tom was a quiet thoughtful man, well over six feet tall, and with his purposeful stride and broad frame always reminded me of a farmer, I guess he was then about 35 years of age. Anyone who asked for help with railway work, would always get an accurate and frank reply, he was always willing to be of help in that direction. We'd been on platform three at Bolton station for only a few minutes when our train arrived on the through road. At the head of the train was a Stanier Class 8F No.**48001** carrying a Nottingham area shedcode. She looked in the pink, the front buffer beam had recently been repainted with a smart coat of red paint, and the smokebox and chimney were newly blacked down. That was all I had time to take in as our train came gently to a stand, as we jumped down off the platform and climbed up into the cab, with the buffers of each wagon clinking into contact all the way down the length of the train. There was only time to exchange a few words with the crew we were relieving, both driver and fireman had their belongings ready and left at once. Looking up at the colour light signal on Bolton West's gantry, there was a green light for us, and we were ready to start. With 35 wagons of coal behind us we started gently, easing the regulator open a little to get all the loose couplings on the stretch, moving forward easily, then, feeling the full weight on our tail, the journey began in earnest with a razor sharp exhaust at the chimney hitting the underside of the bridge which carried the booking hall and offices above. Although the engine had come a good distance, the fire was still in good condition, and it was only necessary to keep filling in the holes and top up under the door. We were well into our stride by Bullfield West, it

was obvious that **48001** had not run many miles since its last shopping. The valve gear was almost silent, and there was no trace of axlebox knock. Another round of firing, about ten or twelve shovels in all produced the right smoke at the chimney top, light grey, and we were travelling fast enough to enable good use of the exhaust steam injector. After opening the main water valve on the tender, the steam valve was swung open, and we could hear the exhaust steam doing its work in the injector in time with the engine's exhaust beat and there were no leaks. We "sailed" over Lostock water troughs picking up about 800 gallons of water, ready to attack the short sharp climb of 1 in 125 up to Chew Moor. Another quick round of firing, mainly to the sides of the firebox would give us enough steam to make the climb. Although there was no difficulty in maintaining pressure, the exhaust injector was turned off in order to leave room for topping up the boiler when descending to Hindley, thus avoiding unnecessary blowing off at the safety valves. Arriving at Hindley, our relief were waiting on the platform, that was the end of the first part for us, but by no means the end of our day. For us, there followed a ride in the brakevan of the train as far as Rainford Junction, and over the now closed and lifted Westwood Park line, this avoided going through Wigan. Up the incline after Pemberton Junction, banking assistance was taken, and I'll always have the memory of that Derby Four barking away behind the brake van and into Orrell tunnel. At Rainford Junction the train slowed sufficiently for us to get off, and also to enable it to safely negotiate the curve round to Randle Junction, where our next job was awaiting us, an empty wagon train bound for the Yorkshire coalfields. Looking back to that day in March 1957, I never actually remember seeing the crew that we were relieving, this was always something of a mystery to me. Contacting my old mate of the day, he was able to tell me that the other crew were in fact, sat in the signalbox chatting to the "bobbie", and had waved to us, acknowledging our arrival. Heading this train of 45 empties was another Stanier Class 8, No.**48158**, a Leeds Holbeck loco. Both dampers were down, but there was a fairly thick, well-burned through fire, and it was well made up under the doors to the level of the lap plate. I always preferred to run with the front damper open, so up came the operating handle, even though some firemen said it made for harder work, because you had to put more coal down the far end of the firebox, and the back one open just a little. With 200lbs per square inch boiler pressure showing on the clock and the water level in the top nut of the gauge glass there was no urgency to put a fire on. Tom was whistling for a road, and with only 45 empties on, we had no where near the weight of the first train. So the firedoors were pulled to, so that the engine's exhaust would beat up the fire, pulling in more air via the dampers under the firebed. In this manner we ambled gently out on to the main line, and, once off the curve it was easier to have another look at the fire to see where the holes were appearing." Only a short climb up through the tunnel, and then its downhill for a good way", said Tom. Obviously, as this was the first time I'd been on a main line goods job I'd need some help that way. I had no route knowledge, and so didn't know when steam demands were going to be greatest. As we trundled along, slowly picking up speed, it was obvious that this engine was not in the same pristine condition as our first one. The thump from the axleboxes was so pronounced that it caused small coal spillage on the footplate to dance up and down. It was almost as comfortable standing as it was sitting, since the continual thump from those axleboxes transmitted itself to the seat on which one might have sat with better mechanical conditions. After the tunnel, we threaded our way cautiously down the other side, through Orrell and past Winstanley Colliery, taking the right hand fork at Pemberton Junction over the Westwood Park branch, firing in readiness for the climb up past Crowe Nest junction and on to Chew Moor, the stiffest gradient being 1 in 97. Time was something that had not entered my head at all, I was enjoying myself on my first main line turn, and the experience would serve me in good stead for years to come. As we drifted down past Lostock Sidings South signalbox the time was a little after 2.50pm and my day

continued on page 38

On the road to Liverpool

The Down Fast and Slow lines between Bolton and Lostock Junction, where the Preston and Wigan lines diverged provided many a thrilling encounter either with a train or sometimes light engine. In this picture taken on June 24th 1961, two Black Fives, Nos. **44940** & **45442** do battle passing Ladybridge, approaching Lostock Junction. The two distant signals in the background belong to Deane Clough. The stream in the foreground was usually called the Middle Brook.   *D. Hampson.*

At Lostock Junction, the line to Preston continues on to the right, whilst the Wigan line swings sharply leftwards and climbs at 1:125 past Lostock Sidings South. The sidings themselves, seen here empty on March 3rd 1963, were laid in the angle of the Preston and Wigan lines during 1915. For many years, during my railway service the sidings were used extensively for storing "cripple" wagons, up to 1,000 could be accommodated.   *D. Hampson.*

At Chew Moor, the next block post, on the line to Wigan, the summit is reached and there is a change in gradient to 1:254 before it falls more steeply past Westhoughton at 1:97. Black Five No. **44989** passes the once busy Chew Moor sidings and the adjacent Westhoughton goods yard, with the 1/47pm Sundays Only train from Bolton to Southport. From here, trains for such places as Bradley Wood on the Calder Valley line would start.   *D. Hampson.*

About a mile before reaching Wigan, Ince is encountered and in these April 1965 scenes is much as it was when rebuilt in 1894. The upper view looks in the Wigan direction, whilst the lower view looks toward Westhoughton. No matter what train I was working, I cannot remember more than a handful of passengers huddled on the platform.   *both British Railways*.

Rainford Junction

Rainford Junction on the route from Wigan to Liverpool Exchange, almost at the end of steam operation on the line. The branch to the left is the one where our empty wagon train with Stanier class 8 No. **48158** at its head was awaiting Tommy Moore and I on that first main line goods trip in March 1957. I never actually saw the men we were relieving, but my old mate of the day assures me that they were sat chatting to the "bobbie" in his cabin. Fairburn 2-6-4 tank No. **42102** of Springs Branch (8F) is in charge of the 13.50 stopping train from Liverpool Exchange to Wigan Wallgate on April 16th 1966.
Chris Spring.

Bolton's Black Five No. **45411** leaves Rainford junction at the head of the 13.15 all stations from Bolton to Liverpool Exchange on April 12th 1966. *Chris Spring*

Stanier Class 8F No **48001**, one of the original domeless boilered 2-8-0's, was still in clean condition and mechanically smooth on that March 1957 coal train to Rainford Junction. Perhaps she had not worked much since her Derby light intermediate repair of November 1956. The loco is pictured on Mansfield shed on August 17th, 1957.
Roy Panting

continued from page 35

was "up" at 3.00pm. Under clear signals at Lostock Junction we gathered up the slack in the couplings and picked up enough speed to take water from the troughs on the fast line. We almost managed to fill the tank which will hold 4,000 gallons. On the outskirts of Bolton we were checked by adverse signals,and crawling into the tunnels after Bullfield East our progress was halted at Bolton West's home signal. "There might be some relief for you at Orlando Bridge", said Tom, I well remember hoping fervently that there would not be, as we were given the road through the station yard. Approaching Bolton West cabin, nestled beneath the lattice girder footbridge which formerly spanned the yard, Bolton East's distant with its electro-pneumatic control rose almost majestically to clear, giving extra hope that there would be no relief. After passing under the station buildings, the safety valves lifted, seeming to scream defiance to anyone intent on boarding for relief purposes. That day, I confess that I felt a great sense of self importance, passing as I was, through my home town of Bolton. It came as a great relief when there was no relief and we spotted Rose Hill's distant also at clear. "You'll be going right through to Todmorden now, more than likely, are you fit? ", said Tom. There was no questioning my eagerness to go on and to enjoy the benefit the two hours overtime would bring. Now,as we rounded the curve past Bolton East was the time to put a good fire on in readiness for the climb to Bradley Fold, after which we could ease off a little. Once clear of Bradley Fold Junction we ran under very easy steam past Radcliffe,

finally shutting off steam allowing the weight of the train to push us through the switch-back of Bury Hollow through Knowsley Street station. On the short, almost level stretch passing Bury L&Y sidings it was time to cram another fire on for the climb of 1 in 85 of Broadfield Bank, and so on to Rochdale where there was still a faint possibility of relief. These uncertainties were quickly dispelled as we ploughed on under clear signals, still firing little and often, through the gentle rise to Smithy Bridge and Littleborough. No more firing now as we plunged into the 2885 yards long Summit tunnel, emerging at the other end we begin our descent of the Calder Valley line to Todmorden, where our relief was awaiting us. On that day in 1957, I felt as though I had been all over the LMS, yet so far as distance was concerned I had not been that far. Now of course came the anticlimax, making our way home, on the cushions, eventually, on the 4.25pm,Rochdale to Southport express back to Bolton shed to sign off duty. Whilst we were walking back to the shed, passing East Junction, the following 4.35pm Rochdale to Blackpool express was approaching from Rose Hill Junction. The train had obviously been stopped or at least severly checked because the engine was being driven fairly hard at slow speed. What was even more memorable, was the sight of compound No.**41102** at the head of the train, the only occasion when I actually saw one of these machines at work on the main line. Regrettably, I was never able to get a firing turn on one of them, and at this time their numbers were diminishing.

I just missed out on the Compound era. The last of Bolton's allocation, Nos.**41101 & 41189** moving to Low Moor (25F) on 17.4.54. The nearest I got to a trip on one of them was a quick look on the footplate of 41186 as she paused for loco duties on Bolton shed with Southport men in charge during 1956/7.Compound No.40937, a Bolton allocation during 1951/2 is pictured on Bolton shed during its stay there.
J. Davenport.

Moses Gate and Green Lane bridge

Looking towards Bolton from Moses Gate with Green Lane bridge about a quarter of a mile distant. Just beyond the bridge in the distance we can see Beehive Mills on the left of the Down Main line, almost immediately after, but out of site was Bolton shed. The variously timed, 10.08am. Brindle Heath to Carlisle Through Freight, with Hughes/Fowler"Crab" 2-6-0 No.**42720** in charge is passing the once busy warehouse. Ex L&Y 0-6-0 saddletank, No.**51408** is hard at work shunting the scrap dock on the Up side. In the left foreground shunter Albert Crowther is ready to operate points and pin down wagon brakes. It was possible at the time to bring a train from Bolton and stop clear of all points in a position similar to the nearest wagon, and run round the train to the other end using the siding shown here overgrown, by the side of Ivanhoe Street on the right. The train could then be shunted, or if required, the train could be drawn across the main line and then propelled into the sidings there.   *D. Hampson.*

Looking back at Moses Gate from Green Lane bridge, this happy group of train spotters give a cheery wave to the crew of a Black Five on an express from Manchester to Bolton. To the right of camera are the carriage sidings where the R.O.F. stock was stored, and from where we started with many a special for Southport. Centre background is Moses Gate's warehouse, and just behind the parachute water column on the left of picture is Moses Gate signalbox. The date is April 1963.
Courtesy Bolton Evening News.

About midway between Moses Gate and Green Lane bridge. Black Five No.**44734** approaches on a Liverpool Exchange to Manchester Victoria stopping train, ready to make its first stop out of Bolton at Moses Gate on June 27th 1961. Immediately left of camera, but out of shot, the railwaymens social club saw many a union gathering.

D. Hampson.

Entering Bolton from Moses Gate

From Green Lane bridge with Beehive Mills to the left, on July 8th 1960, Hughes/Fowler Crab No.**42716** double heads Black Five N0.**45068** on the Colne to London service, timed to leave Bolton at 9.16am.

D. Hampson.

A superbly clear shot from the top of Bolton's coal hopper, taken on July 21st 1968 after closure shows the line from the shed right up to Green Lane bridge. Some steam locos still remain for disposal along with four 0-6-0 diesel shunters which had their fuel drained for use in the Railway Clubs heating system!.

H.L. Holland.

Patriot class 4-6-0 No.**45503** *The Royal Leicestershire Regiment* accelerates past Burnden junction with the 7.35am Aberdeen - Manchester on August 1st 1960. The sidings to the right of the tall home signal guarding the end of the fork line were usually referred to as the "New" sidings, although they were of course a part of Burnden sidings as a whole. *J.Houghton.*

Posing for a photgraphic stop at Burnden sidings are,left to right, Driver Roy Partington (9K) Guard Bill Mc.Elligot,Yard Foreman Lionel Hills & Shunter Joe Ward.
courtesy R.Horrocks

Bolton Burnden Jnc.

Burnden Junction signalbox with its 80 levers controlled movements to and from Bolton shed,and was the box concerned in the incident where, so very nearly there could have been a major accident resulting in both main lines being blocked, see story chapter 8. Burnden Junction signalbox closed in December 1985. *J.Houghton*

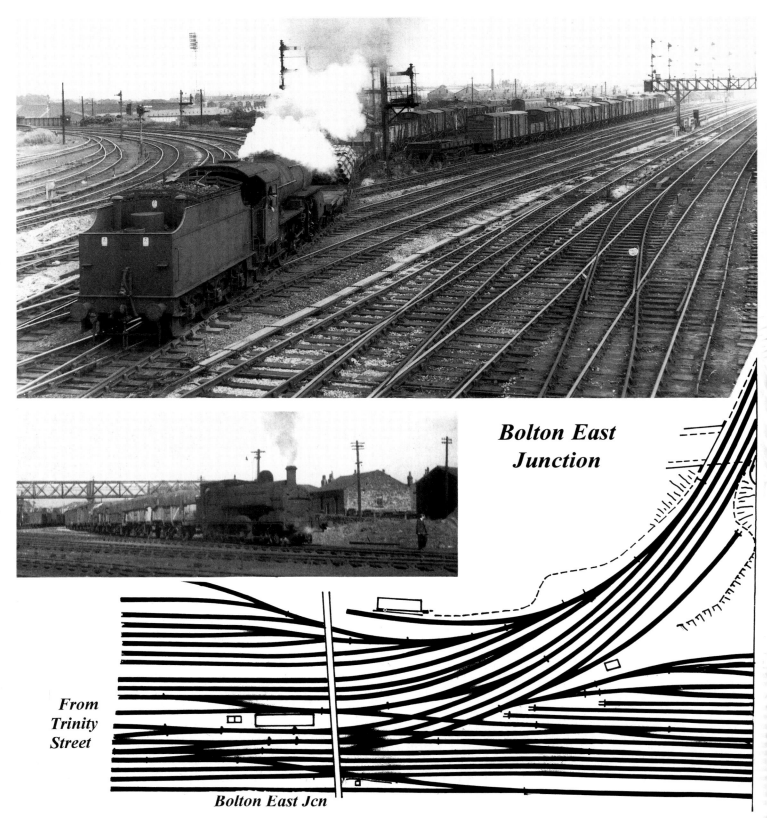

Bolton East Junction

From Trinity Street

Bolton East Jcn

Bolton's Crab 2-6-0 No.**42725** lifts a raft of wagons out of Haslams sidings near Bolton East Junction bound for Halliwell. Leaning over the cab side is fireman Trevor Monk. The discrepancy in engine to tender width is most evident in this view taken on July 26th 1963.   *P. Reeves.*

In the pre diesel era at "B" Side, or Rose Hill sidings, one of Bolton's 0-6-0 saddletanks is busy shunting the yard there. These very old but very capable rebuilds were always master of the work expected of them. Shunter Derek Gregory is on hand as the 0-6-0 drags a raft of wagons up the sidings near to the cattle dock on September 26th 1959. In the background, the footbridge carried many an excited train spotter.   *D. Hampson.*

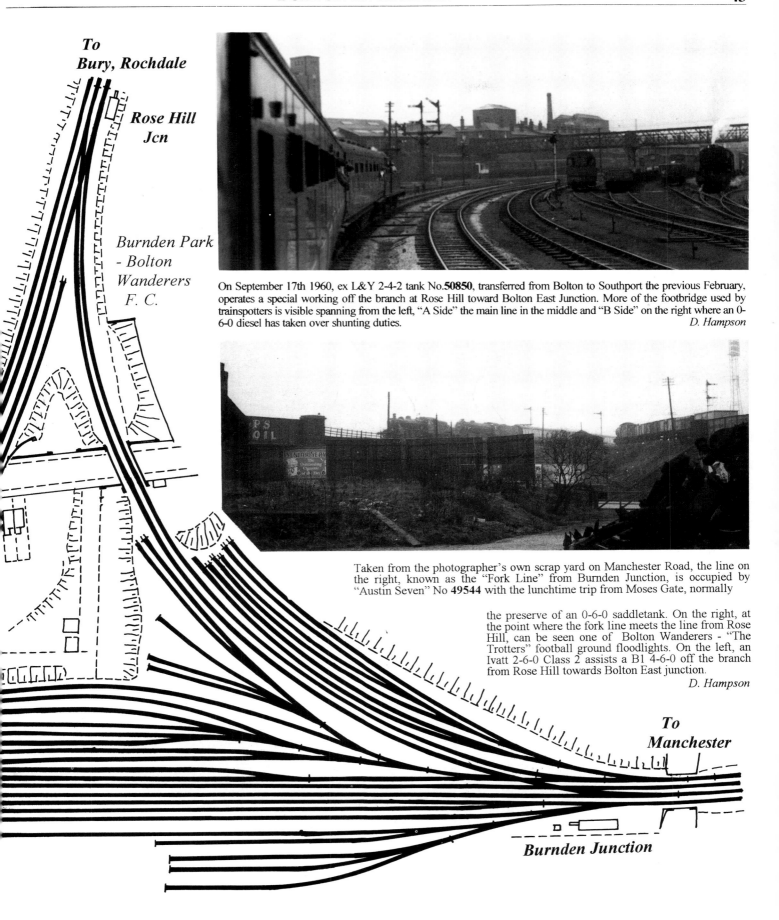

To Bury, Rochdale

Rose Hill Jcn

Burnden Park - Bolton Wanderers F. C.

On September 17th 1960, ex L&Y 2-4-2 tank No.**50850**, transferred from Bolton to Southport the previous February, operates a special working off the branch at Rose Hill toward Bolton East Junction. More of the footbridge used by trainspotters is visible spanning from the left, "A Side" the main line in the middle and "B Side" on the right where an 0-6-0 diesel has taken over shunting duties.   *D. Hampson*

Taken from the photographer's own scrap yard on Manchester Road, the line on the right, known as the "Fork Line" from Burnden Junction, is occupied by "Austin Seven" No **49544** with the lunchtime trip from Moses Gate, normally

the preserve of an 0-6-0 saddletank. On the right, at the point where the fork line meets the line from Rose Hill, can be seen one of Bolton Wanderers - "The Trotters" football ground floodlights. On the left, an Ivatt 2-6-0 Class 2 assists a B1 4-6-0 off the branch from Rose Hill towards Bolton East junction.

D. Hampson

To Manchester

Burnden Junction

Taken from the footbridge spanning the tracks, this view looks back toward Rose Hill Junction with "B Side" to the left. Clearly visible are the floodlights of Bolton Wanderers Football & Athletic Club. Black Five No.**45375** of Southport shed brings the 4/25pm Rochdale to Southport express off the branch toward East Junction. The siding immediately to the right of the train is Haslams, whilst the main line to Manchester is furthest right.

P. Reeves.

The 4/35pm Rochdale to Blackpool express, passing Bolton East Junction on July 26th 1963. The smokebox carries the reporting number 1P61, which I had chalked on No.**45078**'s smokebox before driver Ronnie Horrocks and I left Rochdale that very day. *P. Reeves.*

Bolton East Junction

Approaching Bolton East Junction on the line from Manchester Victoria, Stanier tank No.**42607** of Springs Branch shed is in charge of an express. To the left is the branch to Bury & Rochdale via Rose Hill Junction. On the right of the picture, a rake of empty carriages stands in A Side on July 26th 1963. *P. Reeves.*

Southport's Caprotti fitted Black Five No.**44686** drifts easily past Bolton East Junction with the 5/ 15pm stopping train from Rochdale to Southport on October 3rd 1963. *D. Hampson.*

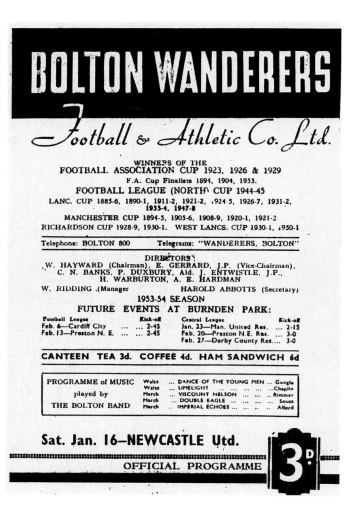

THE LOVE MATC

Almost the exact spot where Arthur Askey (alias driver Bill Brown), and Glenn Melvyn (alias fireman Wally Binns), in the film, "The Love Match", climbed over the fence to watch their favourite team, "City". Actually, Burnden Park, the then home of Bolton Wan-

Rose Hill Junction

...derers, was literally just over the fence. The "box" behind Rose Hill signal box was used on match days to display the half time scores from other football grounds.
Courtesy Bolton Wanderers Football & Athletic Club.

Bolton Trinity Street

Bolton Trinity Street station just as I remember it until the major reconstruction altered its facade for ever. Note the almost total absence of motor cars, Trinity Street seems to be inhabited only by buses on March 7th 1962.   *British Railways.*

(*Above*). A Fairburn 2-6-4 tank with a light train of three bogies ambles into Number Four platform at a deserted Bolton Trinity Street. The date is uncertain, but because the two ventillating cupolas, removed in 1959, are still in place, it precedes that year. The elevated Bolton Station Down Box is clearly shown in the left background. The sidings in the centre foreground lead into "A Side" via Orlando Street ground-frame.   *Les Allen.*

(*Right*). Black Five No.44782 in charge of a Manchester bound express on Thursday September 3rd 1964. Apart from the last two months of its life this loco resided at Agecroft shed during my railway career. Trinity Church dominates the left background, closely followed by the elevated Bolton Station Down signalbox. Clearly visible beneath the box is a repeater signal relating to the Down Goods line signal on the other side of Trinity Street bridge, a signal with a set of catch points protecting the adjacent passenger loop.   *H.L. Holland*

(*Left*) Ivatt No.**43133** is hardly recogniseable as a trial engine. Apart from white smokebox numbers, and distinguishable, large cab side numerals, this Iron Horse has a decidely unkempt appearance standing on Number Two platform at Bolton Trinity Street. A native of Hurlford (67B) she was trialled at Bolton between the 2nd & 16th of April 1963, but was not used on April 12th which was Good Friday. In this scene, No.43133 is almost certainly operating the 3/20pm ex Blackpool Central to Manchester express which was a Bolton turn on Saturdays Only. Driver Jack Byrne is just visible, with whom I worked for a number of weeks in number 2 passenger link in 1960.

Collection S. Taylor.

(*Below*) One of Southport's allocation of BR Standard Class 4MT 4-6-0's No **75019** is captured as it leaves platform 2 of Bolton's Trinity Street station for it's destination, Manchester Victoria. The train is almost certainly the 2.20p.m ex-Southport, as the station clock displays the time as around ten minutes past three. To the right, the stock for the 4.32p.m to Rochdale stands in the bay platform, overlooked by the goods warehouse which dominates the right of this late 1950's scene. *Les Allen*

Collision

at

Bolton West

15th

August

1963

On August 15th 1963, an accident took place at Bolton West Junction on the Down through road. The principle "players" were a light engine, No.**75017**, a class 4MT 4-6-0 of Southport (27C), and an empty coaching stock train from Lightbowne (Manchester) to Kirkdale (Liverpool) comprising 18 coaches, at the head of which was Black Five No.**45339** of Newton Heath (26A). It appears that the signalman at Bolton West, having forgotten about the presence of the light engine which was at a stand at signal, and moreover, had been taking water from the column there, cleared the signals in rear of the light engine for the following empty stock train. A collision took place, resulting in the class 4 being driven forward for some distance and partly de railed. Buffer locking of the two locomotives occurred, and two coaches of the empty stock train were seriously de railed. Bolton shed was advised of the derailment by control at 11.15am and its Tool Van was ready to leave the shed by 11.45am. After waiting 15 minutes at the shed outlet, Mr.Fruish, the

Running Foreman requested its immediate release. Presumably, it had been realised that the Bolton outfit would be inadequate to deal with the situation, Newton Heath's 30 ton crane being sent instead. The B.R.Standard loco had run light engine from Rochdale and was diagrammed to work the 12/30pm stopping train from Bolton to Rochdale. Bolton's Stanier tank No.**42444** was used instead. The driver of the Black Five was not hurt, but the driver of No.**75017** was taken to Bolton Royal Infirmary with a broken arm and head injuries. Both locomotives were temporarily taken to Bolton shed. The Black Five leaving for Crewe works at 5/00pm on 23rd August whilst the BR Standard loco was still at Bolton on September 2nd. Both locos were repaired and returned to traffic. In the two photographs, the Newton Heath crane is seen re-railing the rolling stock, whilst No.75017 has its bogie wheels re-railed.

Both D. Hampson.

Willing workhorses the "Crabs"

The curious, pincer like action of the valve gear on the Hughes/Fowler 2-6-0s earned for them the nickname "Crabs". Whatever else you said about them they certainly were willing workhorses. They were easy to fire, would steam freely and were generally tolerant toward most schools of thought, where driving was concerned. A couple of months after Jack Hartley and I trialled her, No.42873 sports a fair coating of grime at Newton Heath during May 1957.
Roy Panting.

Chapter Eight

As noted elsewhere in most cases, Bolton was the depot that the great majority of works engines, ex Horwich, were trialled at. Those engines that had received General repairs there often stayed for close on a month. Others,which had received repairs of a more minor nature about half that time. During the mid fifties, the total number of locos allocated to Bolton was just about 42, the works engines being heavily relied upon when extra power was required for excursions during the Summer months and for special freight and the movement of empty coaching stock. When I think of the works engines, and Horwich Loco Works, I cannot help but recall immediately the "Crabs", those of Hughes Fowler parentage, although Horwich did in fact repair those of the straight framed and taper boiler variety designed by Stanier. Today, it is well known that the reason for these locos being dubbed with the nickname "Crabs" is because of the ungainly, pincer like action of their valve gear. As school kids we called them "Dippers" because of the "Dip" in the framing over the valve gear. Another and most amusing name for the "Crabs" has recently come to light. "Monkey Jumpers" was apparently a name applied to them during the 1940's when instead of being maintained at Horwich some were dealt with at Crewe, this enabled Horwich to concentrate on wartime tank production. My earliest memory concerning the Crabs is of my seventh firing turn.During late March of 1957 I had signed on for cleaning duties at 12.00 noon. Some time later, I was told to go by bus to Horwich Works, where I was to meet Jack Hartley, my driver, already at the works. The running departments mess room or cabin at Horwich always seemed to have a friendly atmosphere. As you entered by the door at the top end of the hut there was a coal fired stove on top of which there was a large kettle or urn which was kept topped up and on the boil ready for a brew. Down one side there were padded bench seats, opposite which, there resided two or three tables and their chairs. At the opposite end to the door, a small blackboard hung on the wall with details of which engines were to be trialled that day and which of the two drivers were to trial them. Beneath the blackboard there was a small wooden hatch, through which, the superintendent, Mr.Caunce, who resided next door,would pass messages to the locomen. That day

I was greeted as I walked into the cabin, by Jack's cheery smile and was told we were to take **42873** light engine to Bolton, after a short, sharp run tender first to Adlington Junction, just to make sure it wouldn't run hot. By 3.15 we had spread the fire in 42873's firebox and set off, down the works yard toward its West Gate box, whistling for the exit signal, and stopping briefly, by the box to let the signalman know exactly where we were going. On that short tender first journey to Adlington, we gave **42873** a pretty quick run, Jack assuring me that he would make me work hard, all the while reminding me of his nickname, "Slogger Jack from Cairo". Once we arrived in the sidings at Adlington Junction we made a thorough check of all bearing surfaces for signs of overheating. We didn't detect anything untoward so we were able to carry out the instruction to take her light engine to Bolton. Jack was still grinning all over his face and encouraging me to "put plenty on", and when conditions would permit, shoving the regulator right over into second valve. Now **42873** had been given a General overhaul and was a treat to work on, there was no noise at all from the valve gear and she ran particularly smoothly. On arrival at Bolton shed we filled the tender from the coal hopper and dropped on to the ash pit. Just to make doubly sure, we made a final check round for any over-heating, sure enough, our quick run to Bolton had found a problem spot. The left hand eccentric return crank was too hot to touch and would require some attention from the fitting staff before entering revenue earning traffic. When an engine arrived at Bolton after General overhaul or repairs that involved attention to valve gear and axle boxes, it was usual to run them on a few slow turns first of all. A favourite for just that purpose was the bank engine at Bradshawgate just outside Bolton station. Seven miles banking to Walton's siding, mostly at a fairly slow pace,and a nippy run back down the bank to its place of rest, stopping at least once a shift for water from the parachute column at Craddock Lane. During the mid fifties, there were three bank engine turns all in Kearsley Pilot Link, and a further evening turn which signed on at 10.00pm turn 301F in the bottom goods link. Those three turns in the Kearsley Pilot Link were,7.10pm turn number 280, 1.50am turn number 281 (MX) and 8.00am turn number 282 (MSX). For the early evening turn the engine was prepared, so it was just a case of signing on, getting the tools from the stores, a quick check round the engine and fifteen minutes later you were off the shed. Occasionally, you could be in action straight away on arrival at Bradshawgate if the 6.15pm Rochdale to Hellifield needed banking assistance. More often than otherwise though, the Hellifield men on this job with their "Crab" seemed to make light work of almost any load, and it was rare indeed that this train was banked. So, usually, the first job was to back into the siding on the Down side at Bradshawgate and wait events. Usually the first train needing assistance would be Brindle Heath to Carlisle, 8.38pm from Haslams (Bolton) Sidings, having picked up there. This train was a class **D** part vacuum brake fitted train carrying top and right hand headlamps. There was a time when this particular train was banked by the loco which had double headed a parcels train from Accrington with a Black Five, and so the working varied from time to time. It was always to be expected that the 8.45pm Ancoats to Carlisle would need assisting, booked to leave Bolton at 9.47pm approx., where Bolton men had relieved the Newton Heath crew. This job frequently loaded to anything between 35 and 40 vehicles and was fully vacuum braked carrying class C headlamps. Once you were under way banking this train there was no hanging about, it was a heavy fast train and needed a good shove, so you did your best to do that. On some occasions with older and less vigilant drivers, and perhaps an older class of engine on the banker, the train has left the bank engine behind which meant the banker having to follow at a safe distance until it was possible to catch up again. At the time of which I write, the mid fifties, the train engine on this job would be a Carlisle Kingmoor "Crab" or "Black Five". At about 10.55pm we would be joined by the second bank engine, the crew as noted elsewhere, from number three goods link. From this time onwards, every train requiring assistance was taken by each crew in turn, some of which were, Bolton to Colne, Ashton Road to Carlisle, Kearsley to Blackburn, Heaton Mersey to Hellifield, Brindle Heath to Blackburn, Brindle Heath to Carlisle and of course, any specials that might be running. If it had been a busy shift, then, at some point the fire would need cleaning, though there were some occasions when we didn't stir a wheel. Our relief, having signed on at 1.50am, would walk to Bradshawgate to relieve us at 2.30am. Sometimes the first turn would be up the bank, so a little overtime would be made. Just after midnight, the trip from Bullfield would arrive at Bradshawgate with wagons of coal for the NCB yard there, the brake van from this train being deposited on the loop line just lower down than the signalbox. If the evening bank engine crew had not lit a fire in the brakevan stove, then that was the first job for the fireman on the middle turn. The little stoves in those brake vans, after the ashes had been cleared and some "live fire" put in would be red hot in minutes, some shut eye was made much easier. The siding where the bank engine stood was only a few yards away from the signalbox on the opposite side of the main line, and it was from this signalbox, and the signalman there, via the control circuit telephone that we got our information about which trains would require assistance. The people in Control were, like the rest of us only human, sometimes they got it wrong. Often for the class of engine on the job, a particular train did not need a bank engine. But if the engine was in a poor state mechanically, which caused, for instance, excessive slipping, or if the engine was not steaming well, then, obviously the train would stop for assistance. Because of the foregoing, on such occasions, the bank engine crew would be caught on the hop. During periods of inactivity the fire would be allowed to die down, and consequently, the steam pressure would be lower than what was required to bank a train. This meant that the train that had stopped unexpectedly would have to wait several minutes until the banker was ready, resulting in delay on the main line. In the early hours when there was only a small amount of traffic it didn't matter too much, but occasionally a train would be run into the platform road at the disused Oaks station where it would be brought to a stand in order to allow more important traffic to pass. With the early morning mists and general dampness, the rail could be wet and greasy, this often caused severe adhesion problems. One minute you would be going along steadily at about 15 miles an hour when the train engine would slip violently. This in turn threw the weight of the train on to the banker which would then also slip. The train engine, having regained adhesion but then having the full weight thrust upon it would slip again, and so the sequence went on and on, on some occasions until almost the top of the bank was reached. In this manner it often took an hour or so to cover the seven miles up to Walton's Siding with a stop at the Oaks. When banking a goods train, steam would gradually be shut off on the approach to Walton's Siding allowing the train to slowly draw away. If it was a non fitted freight it would creep slowly over the top of the bank and stop short of Sough Tunnel in order to pin down wagon brakes, thus assisting the engine's steam brake in keeping the train under control on the descent to Blackburn. If it was a fully or part fitted freight it would draw steadily away, all the while gaining speed on the now easier gradient, and dive into the darkness of the tunnel to be quickly swallowed up, the only thing visible being the red eye of the guards tail lamp on his brake van. The bank engine would then follow on carefully past the clear home signal, finally stopping behind the ground signal which, once the points had been set would drop to clear, and allow the banker to cross over to the Up line back to Bradshawgate. After stopping behind the ground signal, the headlamps would require changing around, the one at the front end to red and the one at the other end to white. As a fireman doing this duty many times in almost pitch darkness on those still early turns or late evenings the only sounds on those occasions were from the train which had just left us, with the rhythmical clatter from the buffers of its wagons as it braked on the descending gradient, the dull roar from our blower valve and the bubbling sound of a stream with its waterfall, as it too hurried on its way through the night. There at the top of the bank was a super place to be, hardly a sound, clear crisp air, and sometimes dawn just breaking. It was on one such morning that we had banked the 4.8am Brindle Heath to Carlisle, though on this occasion we had a Stanier Class 8F No.**48399**, ex-works from a General overhaul at Horwich, and carrying a Leeds Holbeck shedcode. At this particular time, **48399** was also equipped with a small snowplough, we were tender first up the bank. Coasting back downhill on our way to Bradshawgate we ran normally until just approaching The Oaks. It was just nicely daylight, our speed about 35 miles per hour. At some distance, I spotted a herd of sheep on the line right in our path and shouted across the footplate to my driver Jimmy Bennett. He reacted much too slowly and made only a token application of the steam brake, we ploughed right through the small flock which appeared to be rooted to the spot. I was horrified, as I looked back, one of the sheep upside down, its legs wildly thrashing in the air. We ground to a stop right beside The Oaks signal box, I was almost speechless, yet still managed to voice some disapproval. Jim however just put his forefinger to his lips indicating silence, just as the window of the signalbox was opened by the bobbie. Jim sought his assurance that he wouldn't say anything to "higher authority", not wanting the bother of having to make out a report form, there the matter ended. The third turn of the bank engine signed on at the highly respectable hour of 8.00am(MSX), their first job being to prepare the engine for turn 290F Bullfield Pilot. Often, at this period in time there would be an **A** Class on this job, and oiling the inside valve gear was a dirty job to have to undertake, especially at the beginning of a shift. So just for that purpose, the majority of the older drivers used to keep a spare set of overalls in a locker. These were slipped on over the ones they'd come to work in and removed when the preparation work was completed. By 8.45am these men would be setting off to walk to Bradshawgate, and by 9.15 would have relieved the middle turn. A lot depended on how well to time freight trains ran as to which would require banking first. Theoretically, the first job could be 8.54, Bamfurlong to Halliwell with Springs Branch men on board. Often however, this job with its ex LNW "Super D" would be running late, and the first job would be the 10.08 Brindle Heath to Carlisle class **H**, usually with a "Crab" 2-6-0 at the front. There wouldn't be much time after returning from banking the latter before the 8.38am, Heaton Mersey to Hellifield was knocking about, this turn worked by Bolton men signing on at 4.58am for turn 313F was booked for relief at Bolton at 11.10am by Bolton men on turn 314F. Power for this working was invariably an Aintree 'Austerity' (27B) and loads could fluctuate wildly. On one occasion whilst working this turn we had run with only eight on, one of which was a wagon of cattle which we put off at Whalley. On such other occasions we have been loaded almost to the full, and at the end of one week's work on this turn we ran so early because of the light load, that we were on Hellifield shed before 1.30pm. There, we cleaned the fire, shedded the engine, and left the firebars which we had taken up, to be replaced by the steamraiser. We then walked across to the station, caught the 2.20pm passenger changing at Blackburn, and there the 3.45pm arriving back in Bolton at 4.15pm, by 5.00pm I was back home having only signed on at 10.40am. Quite often, the bank engine would come to the rescue of a train that didn't quite make it. A favourite for sticking just short of Astley Bridge Junction were the previously mentioned Springs Branch men, though I best remember them sticking with the Austerities, not the "Super Ds". They would make a good run at the bank with just under a full load, about 28 or 29 in those days, with wet power station slack, they were heavy, but would shut off steam a little too soon. Realising this, they would re-open the regulator but would then start to slip on the wet or greasy rail, finally stalling. The fact that the curve on to the branch was a fairly sharp one with a 15 miles an hour speed restriction also contributed to slipping. In most cases, when this sort of thing occurred trying to re-start was futile. A vigilant signalman at Astley Bridge Junction would often wire down to Bradshawgate for the banker to come behind, saving unnecessary struggling. The 8.00am bankers docket read *trip shunt and bank as required*, so at 1.15pm it became a trip and shunt job. At this time, the banker was run out of its loop or siding and crossed over to the Up side loop line. Here, a train of empties from the NCB coal yard nearby would be waiting, having been shunted out by Halliwell pilot on its way to shed for loco duties and relief at lunchtime. Arriving at Halliwell, brakes would be pinned down, the engine detached and then run round the train to couple up at the brake van end. Now the train would be shunted and

the empty coal wagons would be shunted on to more empties from the power station, eventually leaving on either, Halliwell to Sharlstown, or Halliwell to Laisterdyke, Bolton's turns 307 & 77 respectively. On Saturdays, Wakefield men would arrive at Bolton shed to pick up an Austerity and work Halliwell to Pontefract. In later years, these empty wagon trains were concentrated on the new yard at Healey Mills rather than the above points. After making up whatever train there might be at Halliwell, the bankers next port of call was Craddock Lane Sidings on the Up side. Here there might be empty wagons from Peers Steelworks to be collected. By about 3.15pm, the last shunts were being made at Burnden Sidings. Whatever train had been brought would be shunted there, the fire well run down, ready for disposal on the shed and personal belongings gathered from the cupboards on the tender faceplate. Once all the shunting operations had been completed, an often used movement by the signalman at Burnden Junction to run us on to the shed would be for us to run on to the fork right road, there, once clear of the points we would come to a stand, the engine was then reversed. The signalman would then set the road for us to run "facing road" or wrong line on to the shed. There was no signal to start this move, but once the points had been set, the "Bobbie" would give us a green flag from the signalbox. Whilst carrying out this move one afternoon at the end of such a spell on the banker we had stopped on the fork, got the flag from the signalbox and set off on our way to the shed. Just as we were crossing the main line I noticed to my utter amazement, an Austerity coming off the shed and approaching us on a collision course from the opposite direction. Quickly, I shouted across the footplate to my mate, Gus Mercer, who was unsighted because of the curve we were on, we came to a dead stand. What had actually happened was this. A set of Agecroft men on an Austerity had rung out to Burnden box to go light engine to Agecroft shed. They had been standing at the shed outlet signal for several minutes when they saw the green flag exhibited from Burnden box, the signalbox they had rung out to. Thinking that this was a signal to pass their shed outlet signal at danger they had started to come off the shed and had found themselves on a collision course with us, the crew that the green flag was actually for. The signalman at Burnden had also noticed what was going on and had shouted to the Agecroft men to go back on to the shed, and, in no uncertain terms had given them "what for". They had had no instructions to pass any signal at danger and were fortunate indeed that no accident had happened. By the time the banker had reached this time of the day, the engine had been off shed for over 20 hours. With the best will in the world mistakes would be made, and a works engine would be put on a job which turned out to be just too fast because the loco was not sufficiently run in. During the Summer of 1961, I was marked with Jack Swarbrick, a spare man at the time to work a special to the Lake District. We had signed on at about 6.30am and our engine was ready prepared for the job, a "Crab" 2-6-0 which was ex works, No. **42920**. We made the usual run to Horwich carriage sidings, via Blackrod Junction, and on arrival, backed on to nine corridor coaches. From the carriage sidings we ran empty stock to Chorley where we made our first stop to pick up. Jack had tried to impress upon me that I'd need to put on a good thick fire as there would not be time to hang about once we got on the West Coast main line. The coal was of mixed quality and contained a high proportion of dust, fortunately, I had at least built the fire right up under the door. In first valve of the regulator, the "Crabs" were pretty weak affairs, but today there there was to be no nonsense. Once we got into our stride after the Preston stop, we were quickly into second valve with the reverser eventually up to 25% with the fire bouncing and the mixed quality coal torn from the shovel at the firehole. With the exhaust injector working almost continuously, and firing over the top of the deflector plate she easily maintained boiler pressure at around 175-180lbs for the greater part of this fairly short journey as we sped on. Although there were few occasions when I was short of steam on a "Crab", owing to their rather low maximum working pressure of 180lbs per square inch, you couldn't afford to let things get out of hand. Anything below 160lbs on the clock, and no doubt about it, you were struggling, the brake was starting to rub causing the driver to use the large ejector to keep it off, which in turn used more steam, hindering matters somewhat. In what seemed no time at all we arrived at Carnforth where our booked relief was waiting for us. We made our way to the Train Arrangers office to see if there was any return work for us, there wasn't. Jack asked if it would be in order for him to refresh the Windermere route, to which, the official gave his ascent, but with the stipulation that the fireman would not be going. Needless to say, the latter instruction was totally ignored, both of us travelling home passenger on the Lakes Express, changing at Preston. The following day I was marked for a goods turn, 6.12am off the shed to work Bullfield to Horwich. The Lakes Express was also booked to run again at the same time as the previous day and with the same engine and driver. Ted Brierley and myself had been stood for some while, backed up to our train at Bullfield with our Black Five No. **44692**, when Jack Swarbrick and his mate on No.**42920** drew alongside us on the slow line. The message was that they were backing inside and would exchange footplates with us, saying that their "Crab" was a "demick". As we wondered why, the "Crab" eventually came alongside and we swapped footplates. The crew on the Crab explained that the metal in the right hand crosshead had "run" on the previous days working. Only at the last minute had the fault been discovered, our Black Five was the only suitable alternative, hence the changeover.

The crew that had taken over what had been our class 5 hurried off to take up their booked work, leaving us to survey the damage to No.**42920**. Looking at the metal which had melted out of the crosshead, it had formed a crust along its entire length, a grey strip about two inches wide and, I suppose about a sixteenth of an inch in thickness which had curled upwards. That day on our slow turn we would manage with it, but no way could it have worked the Lakes special. Ted, nicknamed "Nazzie Ned" because of his vile temper had some pretty course comments to make about "spare" men who failed to oil up properly. In actual fact, if the failure to No.**42920** was due to lack of oil, it wouldn't be Jack's fault since the engine was prepared for us. It could have been lack of sufficient preparation on the return run on the day previous, I never got to the bottom of it. At Bolton during the late fifties and early sixties we had a Saturdays only goods turn for which we signed on at lunchtime, about 1.00pm, Coton Hill to Law Junction. For this we travelled on the cushions to Wigan Wallgate. From there we either walked up the main line to Bamfurlong Sorting sidings, or caught a bus to Abram ending with a short walk to Bamfurlong. On arrival at the latter, we usually awaited this fully fitted in the signalbox. I was only marked twice for this job and on both occasions had a "right ride out" Setting off on the first part of these two with Donny Moores on No.**42852**, a **1A** engine, the "Super D" on the banker had hooked on behind us and would stay with us all the way to Withnell. First of all over the switchback railway with its sharply contrasting gradients, largely due to mining subsidence, past Amberswood West and East and on to De Trafford Junction. Right from the word go, it was evident we were going to have a battle, and it was obvious that the 43 vehicles on our tail were pretty heavy. We were relying on the "D" behind us more than was reasonable, there was little or no life in the fire at all. Stopping at the single line at Whelley, Don sent me back to the box to collect the staff for the single line. I had to suffer being admonished by the signalman, who told me somewhat

Once run in at Bolton on a few slow turns after their visit to Horwich for repairs, the Crabs were ideal power for excursion work. On the occasion of working the special to the Lake District, it does appear that someone neglected to oil the right crosshead, causing the metal to run on No.**42920**, seen here ex works on June 4th 1961 at Blackpool South.
F. Dean.

tiresomly that the banker would carry it. On the fairly level stretch after Adlington Junction, and before Chorley we really leant on the banker, and used the time to knock the fire about in readiness for the climb up the steep section to Withnell. There was a lot of talk that day about Scotch coal in our tender, I just couldn't make her steam at all, and smoke at the chimney was none existent, the coal, once put into the firebox just seemed incapable of burning. As we approached Withnell on that now closed route, the "Super D" pushed even harder in order to loosen the coupling enabling them to un hook and we could hear the shrill piercing whistle from her indicating that we were now on our own. Over the top at Withnell we went, down in the bottom nut of the gauge-glass went the water level with both injectors on. Drifting down towards Cherry Tree Junction and Blackburn, once again we had the fire irons in the firebox. The bent dart to loosen under the door, the long pricker to knock the rest of the fire about. Something like order was restored for the short but fairly hard climb up Cemetery Hill out of Blackburn onwards toward Wilpshire, after which we had another long downhill stretch to Whalley, giving us chance to prepare for the last few miles. Half way down Whalley Bank at Langho was a large house, right beside the lineside, the inhabitents of which always gave a cheery wave when, approaching the spot the crew whistled during reasonable hours. There always seemed to be someone in, and if so, always waved their greeting. Today however was different, we didn't have time to think of pleasantries and both of us were taking turns at firing. By this time both of us were,to put it mildly, a bit fed up, and although we were passing through some of the most beautiful scenery in the country, didn't have time to enjoy it. Hellifield, and our relief couldn't come soon enough as we limped along with the large ejector on by the time we reached Gisburn in order to stop the brakes from going on. As we painfully slowly dragged our train into the sidings at Hellifield, it surely must have been obvious to our relief that all was not well on board our footplate and that we were in "bad nick". It came as no surprise therefore when the Hellifield men refused to go forward with No.**42852**, choosing instead to have the fire cleaned on Hellifield shed.

As we drifted down the bank toward Cherry Tree Junction, on the Saturdays Only Coton Hill to Law Junction working, both Donald Moores and I cursed our ill luck in encountering such a heavy train, an engine in poor condition, and a dirty fire. In this mid fifties view, Horwich Crab No.**42842** has an easy task with a featherweight three coach stopping train toward Preston. The branch to Chorley is in the foreground,with Cherry Tree Junction in the right background.
John E. Porter.

Looking in far better condition than on the Coton Hill to Law Junction trip,which we operated from Bamfurlong to Hellifield,No.**42852** stands quietly at her home shed,Willesden (1A). Not long off the shops she also carries BR A.W.S. equipment in this photo on Sunday March 19th 1961. *Roy Panting.*

Blackburn to Hellifield

Whalley viaduct with its 48 spans set amidst some of the most beautiful countryside in the North of England. But with No.**42852**, a dirty fire and an engine that would not steam we had no time to enjoy it. With 43 wagons on our tail on that day during 1959, we had enough on our plate coaxing steam from an unwilling boiler.   *F.Dean*

(*Centre*). Stanier 2-6-4 No.**42624** comes off "The Lanky" on the approach to Hellifield Station. Immediately behind the train is Hellifield Low Level sidings where our freight trains were often re marshalled before setting off toward Blackburn. The line to Skipton curves sharply away to the left
                    Collection G. Robinson.

(*Lower*) Waiting a little further on, Caprotti fitted Black Five, No.**44741** stands at the northbound platform at Hellifield with a connecting train in rear. To the left Hellifield shed nestles at the foot of the hills with a Derby Four on a short freight in front.
                    Collection G. Robinson.

Banking trains from Bradshawgate up the seven or so miles to Walton's siding could be an arduous business, the going was often slow, sometimes only 10 - 15 miles an hour. Once past Astley Bridge Junction there came the stiffest part of the climb 1:72. Interestingly, the goods warehouse at Halliwell is just visible through the third and fourth arches of Tonge Viaduct as a Stanier Class 8F lifts a Brindle Heath - Carlisle freight up the bank circa 1967.

P.Salveson

Banking Duties from Bradshawgate

On a Summer morning in 1959 during a lull in banking operations at Bradshawgate on the line to Blackburn. The three standing on the signalbox verandah are, from the left, signalman Jimmy Morris, quite a character, in a dry sort of way a comedian too. One Summer Saturday evening, Jim arrived at the box somewhat late for the late shift, he was surprised to find the stationmaster in attendence. On his way to work Jim had stopped for a "quick half" followed by fish and chips, which he was in the process of consuming on arrival. Somewhat embarrassed by the presence of officialdom he was almost lost for words, Thrusting the hand containing newspaper and chips toward the official he asked "Want a chip"? Jim also like to go around using 'nom de plumes'. When arriving at his holiday hotel often signed in as Colonel & Mrs.Morris. In the centre of the group is guard Sam Weatherall. When this picture was taken the time was around 7.45am and Sam would have signed on at about 5.30am to work the 6.20am Bullfield - Halliwell trip, afterwards making his way back to Bradshawgate on foot ready to work Bolton ballast, the brakevan for which would have been left in the permanent way yard there. Sam was one of the very few Bolton guards whose route card was signed for London. To the right is driver Davies, Edwin, to put it mildly was somewhat round. Having got down on his back on one of the benches in the brakevan for five minutes shuteye, he always had great difficulty heaving himself. Hailing his fireman he would shout "Here, lift mi up". Sometimes with raw recruits he would demand, "Here, just give mi shoes a polish" Because of his large size, Edwin was aptly named "Cir cumference". ....!

Author

"Derby 4" 43981
The Bradshawgate Banker

(*above*). The footplate of right hand drive Midland 0-6-0 class 4F No. **43981** as we wait in the bank engine siding at Bradshawgate just outside Bolton station.
Author.

(*right-upper*) Ex Midland 0-6-0 No. **43981** stands in the bank engine siding next to Bennetts coal yard at Bradshawgate circa 1959.
Author

The Oaks

(*right-lower*) On reaching The Oaks, a little over a mile further on, if the trip was proving a difficult one, and slipping due to a wet or greasy rail was encountered, you were glad of a little respite on being turned into the platform road there, in order to let faster moving trains pass. A Carlisle - Brindle Heath train with Black Five No. **45451** in charge is seen passing the station in the early 1950s.
Authors collection

Entwistle Viaduct

Carrying the railway 120 feet above Bradshaw brook, Entwistle viaduct, about 5½ miles from Bolton and about 1½ miles from the top of the bank, but still very little let-up in the gradient 1:74. A Stanier class 8F works a North-bound freight over the viaduct in the mid 1960s.   *P.Salveson.*

The Bradshawgate banker was an ideal turn for running in engines which were ex-works. About seven miles uphill, mostly at a fairly slow pace, then a smart run back to base at Bradshawgate light engine. If there was a possibility of some bearing surface running hot this would expose it. In this 1959/60 picture, Fleetwood's No.**42841** has been outshopped from Horwich with what appears to be a General overhaul, though the locomotive's tender has retained the older stile of BR emblem, possibly on the grounds of economy. From a study of further photographs of this engine it would appear that this older emblem was retained until at least the locos next visit to Horwich for overhaul which came at the end of 1962. After its customary trial period on what was No.42841's last visit to Horwich, the loco returned to the Fylde Coast on the 11/22pm Bolton Blackpool goods on January 25th 1963. The engine is seen here banking a loose coupled freight near Turton. Bolton driver Harry Harrison is at the controls.
Authors collection.

BRITISH RAILWAYS
ENTWISTLE

Entwistle to Walton Sdgs.

(*Above*) With its elevated signalbox and island platform, situated up in the hills, where the gradient is about 1 in 74, the bleak outpost of Entwistle is approximately 1½ miles from the top of the bank. Often, when banking the fully fitted Ancoats to Carlisle freight, instead of taking the through line beneath the signal box, we would race through the platform road, the points having been left set in that direction after the passage of the preceeding passenger train.
Collection S. Taylor.

(*Lower*) Not far to go now to the top of the bank at Walton's Siding as Crab No.**42787** operates a northbound freight past Entwistle on July 4th 1963. In all probability, the train is the 6/15pm Rochdale to Hellifield (SX) with Hellifield men at the controls.
D. Hampson

Days Out on Derby 4's

Chapter Nine

If ever I had a weak spot where firing was concerned, it was the "Derby Fours" of class 4F, both Midland and LMS variety. But with the benefit of hindsight, I'm absolutely convinced that the cold runs were not always my fault. Usually, the "Derby Fours" we worked on at Bolton were those that had been repaired at Horwich Works. Theoretically, they ought to have been in good nick, but it seemed at the time that this was not always so. Why all the cold runs then?. Well, frequently we would have one of these ex-works Derby Fours on the bank engine just outside Bolton station. With a couple of exceptions, the bank engine turns were in Kearsley Pilot Link which encapsulated drivers who had opted to come off main line work and its associated rigours, in favour of a more easy life on a restricted route basis. Drivers from other sheds often remarked that when banked by men from Kearsley Pilot Link they got hardly any assistance at all. This seemed even more so when there was a Derby Four on the banker. The drivers often made the mistake of "nursing" them too much, working them far too lightly, thinking that they were helping their fireman and making his job easier. In fact, by notching the gear up too far they were doing quite the opposite. On a Derby Four it was necessary to keep a lively fire, so they needed to be driven a bit hard. This meant that you didn't notch the valve gear up more than about one and a half or two turns of the reversing wheel. One Summer Saturday evening during 1958, I'd signed on with Noey Howarth at 7.40pm for turn 258F, the bank engine, and together we walked to Bradshawgate to relieve the earlier turn. As we walked through the permanent way yard at Bradshawgate, I caught my first glimpse of our engine for that shift. Standing in the siding, on the other side of the main line, tender first up the bank and fresh from overhaul at Horwich was No.**44504**, my heart sank."Hell", I thought to myself."A Derby Four, and wrong road round as well". I never liked banking tender first, the gradient played tricks with boiler water levels showed in the gauge glasses. Occasionally, it was prudent to be tender first up the bank, especially when the weather was wet from the South West. The crew we were relieving didn't hang about, after all it was Saturday night, and still not too late to get a pint or two. Climbing up on to the footplate we checked that boiler water levels and fire were ok, stowed our gear in the cupboards on the tender, and then made our way to the signalbox, up its six or seven steps to keep the "bobbie" company. Saturday nights on the banker were usually quiet affairs, the 7.00pm(SO)Bury to Hellifield would have gone up the bank well before we arrived. Later on there was the possibility that Brindle Heath to Blackburn would need banking. Some of the older hand drivers used to tell of this job being double headed and banked as well, so heavy were its loadings. By this time however, loadings had dwindled somewhat, and from the records that I have, I note that on May 24th 1958, the train had left Brindle Heath at 11.5pm with 16 on and picked up at Haslams (Bolton) Sidings at 11.35pm, finally leaving with 41 on equal to 50 of mineral at 12.5 on the Sunday morning. On this occasion with "Austin Seven" No.**49674** at the head of the train though assistance would be taken, certainly no double heading would be required. That evening, as we sat chatting to the signalman at Bradshawgate, it had just nicely started to go dark, the gas lamps in the cabin had just been lit and we had decided, whilst all was quiet, that we would partake of our supper.

Minutes later, a message came through on the circuit telephone saying that a "Special Passenger" from Paignton, and bound for Colne had left Midland Junction with ten on and was now passing Kearsley. The class 6P would require banking assistance to Walton's siding. The signalman of that day, Maurice Blackburn, a very good railwayman, was quick to point out to Control that the banking of passenger trains up this particular bank was not authorized. Consequently, we would have to double head the special, and we decided that before doing so, we would turn the engine on the triangle, so as to be engine first up the bank. Running engine first over Johnson Street connecting line and beneath the tunnels of Newport Street, we were then able to reverse, and run tender first, facing road into number 3 platform where the special had arrived. My disappointment was extreme when I noted that power for the special, although a class 6P was not the expected "Jubilee". Instead it was a "Crab" 2 6 0, No.**42944**, that was the only 6P we would see that night. Carefully, we buffered up to the train engine and threw our tender shackle on to the front hook of the "Crab's" draw-gear. Next came the difficult task of coupling the two vacuum pipes together, so that we had a continuous automatic brake. The fireman on the "Crab" had taken off his headlamps, and I put express headlamps at the smokebox end of 44504. During the time we had spent turning our engine I had been busy building up the fire. Now that we were almost ready to leave, dark grey smoke was hurrying off the top of our chimney into the now much darker night sky, the blower valve helping it on its way into the atmosphere. The crew of No.**42944** were expecting us to go through with them to Blackburn, but because Noey was on a restricted route availability this was not possible, and so he went to great pains to ensure that the train crew were aware that we would stop and detach at Walton's Siding, the top of the bank. I couldn't keep the safety valves quiet for much longer now, the boiler was getting full. Luckily, we got the tip from the station staff and a green light from the guard with the needle on the pressure gauge close to the red mark. A quick glance to make sure we've got a road, a pop from each engine whistle and we were off, so was the injector, I wondered apprehensively how we would fare. There was no time to be nervous now as we strode over the junction past West box and stormed into Bradshawgate tunnel. Once we were out of the other side of the tunnel it was time to put a quick round of firing on, about four down each side, fill up under the door and two under the brick arch. Crash, the firedoors were slammed shut as we blasted our way past the switched-out Craddock Lane signalbox, and wonder of wonders, the safety valve lifts, on went the exhaust steam injector. "Steady Jim", said Noey, quickly adopting a guiding influence."We don't want to get back to Bradshawgate with a boxfull of live fire". I couldn't believe it, we were doing our share, working hard, the engine was steaming well, and the crew on the "Crab" were hardly blowing the smoke off their chimney top. I lifted the firing plate into position, and firing lightly in short bursts we were able to maintain almost full pressure most of the way up the bank, the exhaust steam injector was on for the most part. There used to be a saying amongst locomen that you only needed to show it the shovel and it would steam. That night was no exception, and Noey, a man of many years experience, voted No.**44504** the best Derby Four he had ever worked on. On

The best Derby Four that I ever worked on. When we got "a good un", we used to say, "She'll steam wi' bricks in't box". No **44504** certainly wasn't steam shy after her General Repair at Horwich. The night Noey and me had her double heading the special up the bank, it was a "play job". We could have gone on indefinitely. The 0-6-0 is pictured on Llandudno Junction shed on one of the outside roads.   *E. N. Neale*

that occasion, everything was in our favour, a clean fire, good coal,and a good engine expertly handelled. Some weeks later however, things were very different with another specimen of the class. It was Preston holiday time,and signing on at 7.59am for C895 special, Jack Cleary and myself made our way round to No.**44390** on number nine road. The sun was well up in the sky and it was certain to be "a scorcher". Just our luck to find No.**44390** sporting a tender cab, it certainly was going to be "a scorcher" in more ways than one. Looking back to that Monday morning, we should have had the fire cleaned before leaving the shed. Alas, we didn't, thinking that we would manage, it was a big mistake, if only we knew what was to follow. This particular Derby Four had been given repairs at Horwich, but was pretty well run in. Some time after leaving the shops for its trial at Bolton, the engine had been involved in a de railment whilst working the carriage shunt at Horwich. This had neccessitated a quick return to the works to have things put right with its damaged brake gear, before again coming to Bolton to resume the trial period. We ran first of all, light engine to Horwich carriage sidings via Blackrod Junction, and backed on to nine non corridor coaches, often referred to as nine wide sets, their compartments being the full width of the bogie. During the short trip from Bolton it became obvious that the fire was in pretty bad condition, and we learned afterwards, that she had in fact been in steam all of the weekend previous. From Horwich we ran empty stock to Chorley, where we made our first stop to pick up passengers. Before getting the right-away, we just about managed to fill the boiler and coax the needle on the steam pressure gauge round to its maximum of 175lbs per square inch. To make matters worse, the quality of the coal left a lot to be desired, there was some coal, but briquettes, coal eggs and a large amount of dust seemed to form the bulk of fuel available. The sun was hotter now as we drifted down Chorley Bank beneath the flying arches. The dust from the coal eggs and briquettes was swirling around the tender shovelling plate area like a mini sandstorm into the cab, some

of the finer stuff finding its way on to ones face giving a feeling of something akin to sunburn in its worst form. Use of the hose pipe hardly seemed to help, it simply carried the dust out of the tender on to the area below the tender shovelling plate. If I shovelled it into the firebox, because of the high water content it made things worse, damping down the fire. Much of it ended up on the ballast, but was quickly replaced by more of the same variety, as the tender was arranged to be as self trimming as possible. The more you sweated on the footplate, the more the dust stuck to your face, it was a viscious circle. After Euxton ROF station we made a determined effort to shake up the fire with the doors fully shut, the regulator at full throw and the valve gear out to 75% cut off, its maximum, for a short burst. If we had shifted anything there should have been a dust cloud in the sky, there wasn't, so the fire was worse than we had thought. This treatment had hardly moved anything, except a lot of water from the boiler, after closing the regulator, the gauge glass showed less than a quarter full. Even though we were on a favourable gradient, our speed was so low that we hardly needed to brake for the speed restriction round the curves at Euxton Junction, but whilst coasting, we had both feeds on, and were doing our best to coax more steam from an unwilling boiler. Firing carefully, avoiding putting too much under the brick arch, and keeping the firehole doors closed as much as possible we tried to get things under control. Even so, after the junction we still had only half a boiler of water and about 160lbs per square inch on the pressure gauge, off went the injectors, and on went a quick round of firing. We made a determined attempt to get the train moving again, and made good use of the falling gradients, all the while manipulating the injectors on and off according to steam demand, and in this manner we eventually drifted miserably into Preston with 120 on the clock, the water in the bottom nut of the glass and the big blower on to keep the train brakes from applying. Another problem now manifested itself, ash from the ashpan was blowing up, through the floorboards and into the cab. Some of the stuff found its way into our eyes, but no matter how much we swilled down on the footplate there was no end to it, so we had another discomfort to put up with. There was no way we could even contemplate slightly closing the damper,we needed every bit of air that might be coming in through the firebed. We made valiant efforts with the fire, knocking it about with the fire irons, loosening it under the door with the dart, and dragging some of it from under the brick arch with the long Lanky pricker. Until something like order had been restored, there was no way we would leave for Blackpool Central.Fortunately, we were booked for a rather longer than usual stop at Preston, but the signals did seem to be off for us for a good while before we eventually got under way. The journey to Blackpool Central via the Marton Line was no better than the first part of the working. It was the same story, the steam and water levels see-sawing up and down, both competing for the lowest position. There were a lot of questioning looks on the faces of the passengers that day as they passed our footplate at Central station for their day of fun on the beach. I felt like burying my head in the sand on which they would probably be walking later on. Once the stock had been put to one side we had just enough time to turn the engine on Blackpool's electric turntable, back up again, this time empty stock headlamps were carried, back through Preston,and round Farington Curve,re entering Preston for another quick "dash" to Blackpool. The way things were going it had become a right nose bag job, snatching a sandwich and a swig of tea from the bottle on the hob over the firedoors. After this

continued over

second express "dash" to Blackpool the fire was so dirty it was "burning" a blue colour, just like whinberry pie, but so tight were the timings we had little or no time to spare after turning the engine once more. Once we had coupled up to our stock, I made a desparate attempt to clear some of the clinker that was obviously present. Trying to penetrate the firebed was well nigh impossible. We had a good quality Lanky pricker on board, but when I tried to stab it into the clinker it seemed to sink into the top inch which was of a sticky consistency, below that it was like granite. In the end I was forced to give it up, our battle against time was lost. In trying to get to the firebars we had thrown out so much live fire that the position now seemed even worse, the firebox having cooled down a good deal. There was no use trying any more, we were late away, and the way things stood, there was little enough prospect of making up any lost time. There was at least one thing, we could tell our relief that we had tried to clean the fire with some degree of honesty, after turning yet again round by Lostock Hall and Farington Curve. Our relief didn't know as yet what was in store for them, but they obviously fared no better than us. Three weeks later,

I saw the driver, Wilf Whitehead, who had relieved us, and of course, the inevitable occurred when he accused me of telling untruths, ah well!!!. As previously mentioned, the Derby Fours had a problem with ash coming up from the ash pan, and blowing through the floorboards into the cab. Here, it found its way on to clothing, and, much more painfully, into eyes. I well remember one of the Midland variety of this class arriving on Bolton shed on its way to Horwich Works. Instead of being put on a shed road it was stabled over toward where the coal stack was on number 15 road. On this particular day I was working as steamraiser, and had climbed on board to check water and fire levels. To my amazement, I noticed that someone had placed huge sods of earth around the footplate in the area of the faceplate where the pipework came through the floorboards. I was just starting to heave them overboard when a driver came on to the footplate to prepare the engine, he explained to me that they were there to help prevent ash entering the cab from the ashpan. During wet conditions, even though you were right way round for the weather, the Derby Fours could be relied upon to leak water through their cab roof. Such was the position

By sheer chance, the photographer has captured our "cold" run on that sunny Monday in 1958 as we propelled our stock out of the platform at Blackpool Central with "Derby Four" No **44390**. All the signs of that "cold" run are evident; not so much as a whisper of smoke at the chimney, not even the slightest hint of a white "feather" at the safety valves; and look at the fine coating of dust along the footplating, boiler top and tender cab roof. *F. Dean*

After its last visit to Horwich works for intermediate repairs, LMS class 4F 0-6-0 No.**44525** is pictured at Blackpool Central shed on January 14th 1963. The usual trial period at Bolton had been completed and the loco worked into Blackpool in the early hours of January 11th 1963, with the previous evening's 11/22pm Bolton to Blackpool freight. A Llandudno Junction engine, No.**44525** is credited as the last of the class to be withdrawn in 1966.
F.Dean.

of the join in the cab roof extension, that it could be expected to leak very reliably down the back of ones neck. It did not seem to matter if they were ex works or not, with monotonous reliability, they all leaked. In common with many other anomalies, the locomen had a remedy, soap. At this particular time, we used to receive an issue of soap from the stores, a suitably sized chunk of about two inches square. Now this kind of soap was pretty hard, and on finding a leak in the cab roof, the fireman would climb up to a suitable vantage point, and armed with the soap, would rub some of it into the leaking joint, guaranteed to last for at least one shift. During the Autumn of 1959 I'd signed on with Bob Croston, a spare man at the time, at 7.30am for a special, empty ballast wagons from Bullfield Sidings to Leek Brook in Staffordshire. On this occasion, power for the job was No.**44358** (5D), another Derby Four and ex-works now, after its trial period working its way back to its home depot. From Bolton shed we ran tender first to Bullfield Up Sidings, picking our guard up at Orlando Bridge, the guards signing on point. Sixteen empties was no load to worry about, but running to Manchester under easy conditions, we couldn't get the boiler to steam. There was nothing wrong with the fire, and there was smoke at the chimney, why then wouldn't it steam? Anxious glances were cast at the pressure gauge as we attacked the steep climb out of Manchester Victoria up to Miles Platting. No sooner had we started to work the engine harder,

and draw some air in through the firebars she started to steam a treat, now, it was a piece of cake. So long as you kept the fire built up under the doors, and the corners filled, there wasn't going to be a problem. Here was the sort of situation where I felt I could have gone on all day, but Bob had wired "EGER"(the code word for conductor required) from Heaton Norris Junction, not knowing the road from thence forward. At Denton Junction we came to a stand after a fairly lengthy wait at Ashton Moss Junction. From the former point, Control had arranged for us to exchange footplates with Edgeley men on and Denton Ship Canal with No.**73127** at its head. This latter short trip took us only as far as Miles Platting, where we were unexpectedly stopped by a set of Agecroft men who relieved us there. Further orders were sought from Control and we were instructed to relieve Adswood to Brindle Heath with No.**73125**. A lasting memory of both those Standard class 5's with the Caprotti valve gear was the amount of big end knock they had, and of a variety quite different to any other encountered. On arrival at Brindle Heath with the latter train, the Yard Foreman said he had been told that we were to take the engine on to Agecroft shed and from thence to make our way back to Bolton. However, Bob countermanded those orders telling the foreman to let the signalman know we would be going light engine to Bolton, where we arrived much quicker with just a full eight hours duty.

(*Upper*) Trains from Blackpool, off the Marton Line not requiring to call at Kirkham Station were able to use the flying junction, facilitating their passage through Kirkham, as Jack Cleary and I had done on C895 special with No.**44390**. However, on that day we did little flying, it was mostly crawling. *F. Dean.*

(*Lower*) On the same day that we had our good trip on Derby Four No.**44358**, with empties for Leekbrook we encountered B.R. Standard class 5 4-6-0 No.**73125** on Denton to Manchester Ship Canal. The same loco is pictured operating an up class F express freight not fitted with continuous brake at Leyland. *J. Davenport.*

Chapter Ten

Ivatt 4's "Iron Horses"

The Ivatt Moguls numbered in the series 43000 + 43161 were known to us at Bolton as "Iron Horses". They had been dubbed thus owing to the large amount of steel piping used in their construction rather than copper. Today, in the enthusiast press, I see that the engine preserved in this class, No.**43106**, is referred to by the name "Flying Pig", how it got that name I'll never know and I'll never be reconciled to it. It is well known that these machines were built in response to a demand for more power in the class 4F range. Rather than build more 0-6-0's of Midland parentage, Ivatt insisted on the 2-6-0 wheel arrangement,and took the opportunity of modernising the machine. Really, the only likenesses the Ivatt engine shared with the Midland variety were the slope of the firegrate, 1 in 4, and the wheel diameter, five feet three inches, after that, all likenesses ceased. These locomotives were also the forerunner of the B.R. Standard types of the same class and power, and with their raised footplating over the driving wheels, and outside Walschaerts valve gear they were a thoroughly modern looking engine. The early steaming troubles associated with their double chimneys when first introduced in 1947 are well tabulated in more technical publications, so there is no need for me to go into great detail. By the time I got to work on these machines, the double chimneys had all been replaced with a suitable sized appendage of the single variety. Because of the steep slope to the firebox, it was no good just chucking coal willy-nilly into the firebox, care was needed. The tendency was to fire them more under the door, keeping the back corners well filled, and just now and again, a couple down the far end. Just as with the Derby Fours, if the space between the firegrate and brick arch became restricted, proper combustion would not take place, so you struggled. You could of course, on this class, shake the rocking grate, and just take the chance of the mechanism jamming up, that at least was an advantage over the Derby Fours. If you could make the Iron Horses smoke they would generally make steam, if not, then there was something wrong. On their footplates there was plenty of room in the Ivatt cab, and the tip-up seats of wooden variety were as comfortable as anything else fitted to LMS engines. Both injectors were thoroughly reliable affairs fitted with monitor cones, and in my experience never gave any trouble at all. There was never the problem as on the Stanier 2-6-4 tanks where the injectors were a persistent source of trouble, continually knocking off with much waste of water. Whether driving or firing, visibility was particularly good, either engine or tender first, and I always liked that feeling of being "perched" high up, with wheels and valve gear in full view. When driving, there was no difficulty reading the cut off marking on the sector plate which was slightly inclined and therefore easy to see. Because of their large diameter piston valves these engines ran very freely, and for a loco with only a five foot three inch diameter driving wheel had a fair turn of speed.

(above) Finished in plain black livery, just as she was when first built in 1950 at Doncaster. No.**43069** has been overhauled at Horwich. In common with other locos of the class from the North Eastern Region, the cab side numerals are of a larger variety. The tender is fitted with single line tablet catching apparatus, and the engine stands on number 12 road at Bolton shed awaiting its next duty in the Summer of 1960.

Author.

(Upper) Ivatt Mogul ex Horwich works and of Devons Road Bow shed appears to have had a light repair only. The later B.R.emblem has not been applied, and the loco has a generally grubby appearance on number one road at Bolton shed during March 1959 whilst on trial there.

J. Davenport

In filthy condition, Ivatt class 4MT 2-6-0 No.**43135** of Dawsholme shed (65D) awaits her turn to enter the erecting and repair shops for what possibly was to be her last overhaul on September 16th 1962. The Mogul must have been away from its home shed for some considerable time, for, on November 2nd 1962, presumably following or during her trial period at Bolton, the engine was recorded in the stopped engines book as being sent back to Horwich to have the left leading crank pin re-metalled. Later in the same month, No.43135 was the subject of a vacuum test back at Bolton, on the 22nd in fact, when a blockage was was found and cleared. On November 26th, things must have been sorted out, for the loco left Bolton, light engine to Agecroft with a set of that depots men in charge. No.43135 was withdrawn from service from Manningham (55F) in November 1966, and cut up by Drapers of Hull in January 1967. *P.Claxton.*

Southport Excursion
with 43010

Once the Ivatt 2-6-0's had had a few trips locally, after their visit to Horwich works, they were ideal power for some of the shorter excursion work to Southport or the Fylde Coast. One sunny Monday morning of the Bolton September holiday of 1958, I was marked up for firing on a special day excursion to Southport. My driver that day was a passed fireman, Jimmy Jones. Jim was an ex Plodder Lane man on the LNW side of Bolton, and had transferred to our depot prior to closure of the latter depot. He was an interesting person to fire for, had an excellent knowledge of many things, and in particular was a very good engineman. On this particular trip, our engine was No.**43010**, an Ivatt class 4, 2-6-0 which was ex-works following a General overhaul at Horwich. She was off the shops several days and getting nicely run in. After signing on, we collected the usual bucket of tools from the stores, complete with shovel and headlamps. We made our way round to number 8 road where No.**43010** stood outside the shed by the water column ready prepared for us. Everything was in order for us on the footplate, so after placing light engine headlamps on the front and rear buffer we made our way up the shed yard with mud taps open, water and steam issuing from them. After ringing out to Burnden Junction signalbox, we were signalled off the shed with the top peg,and once clear of the points, ran facing road down the Goods Loop to Moses Gate where our stock was awaiting us. Our guard had made his way to Burnden,and on our way we had picked him up. On arriving at Moses Gate, there were nine non corridor coaches waiting for us,and after quickly coupling up and successfully creating the necessary 21 inches of vacuum in the train pipe, empty stock headlamps, one on the right and one on the middle were displayed for the short run up to Bolton, again, along the Down Goods Loop, this time of course, right road. There were a good many passengers waiting on the platform for us at Trinity Street station, and our first job was to change the headlamps again, this time to express ones, one over each buffer. It was obvious Jim's family were travelling with us that day, so we would have to be on our metal and make sure that we ran to time. Leaving Bolton station behind, and once clear of the tunnels beneath Newport Street, and Moor Lane, we were soon into our stride, though any fast running would have to wait until we had called at all stops to Wigan Wallgate. There was no doubt that No.**43010** was in good order and was riding like a coach over that flat terrain between Parbold and Blowick, our maximum speed would, I guess, be in the region of 70 miles an hour or so. As they passed our footplate, there were some happy smiling

A Ribble double decker bus waits at Parbold's level crossing gates as BR Standard Class Four 4-6-0 No **75046** enters the station at the head of a Southport bound train. This was the location where the last coach of our Bolton to Southport excursion caused lengthy delays to road traffic whilst we awaited assistance following the failure of our Ivatt 2-6-0.   *Jim Peden*

The station at Parbold was well sited for the village and like a great many rural locations, possessed facilities intended to satisfy the requirements of the community. The buildings seen here on the Wigan bound platform arrived progressively over the years as the line and its usage developed. Latterly, the corrugated shelter to the left was intended for the storage of cycles. The canopied waiting room demonstrated the standardisation policies followed by the Lancashire & Yorkshire Railway around the turn of the century. A Booking Office was sandwiched between the Waiting Room and the stone built Station Master's House, this latter structure daiting from the opening of the line in 1855. Parbold Cabin, named in that individualistic way so liked by the L&Y, controlled; and still does, both road and rail movements through the village, giving the signalman a position of some signifigance. A station subway located beneath the ends of the platforms, defies detection from all but the closest of quarters.   *R. D. Foster*

Parbold

between
Wigan
and
Southport

(*Upper*) Although the Stanier Crab was a more modern machine than the Hughes variety.it was not as comfortable for the fireman.Their wooden hinged seats formed the top of an oil cupboard and were arranged close to the cab side sheeting.You could, therefore,only get one cheek on them.Stanier Straight Framed Crab No.**42977** operates a stopper over Hoscar troughs on the line from Wigan to Southport on August 5th 1964.

Brian Barlow.

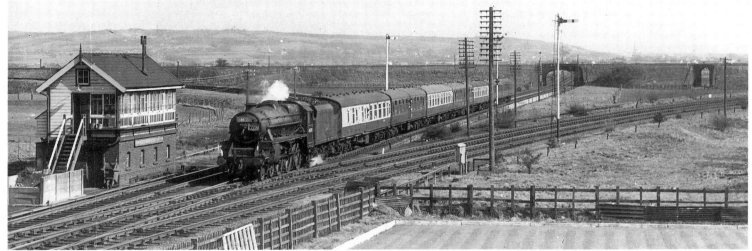

(*Centre*) Expresses from either Wigan or Southport were well into their stride by the time they reached Burscough Bridge with its leftwards connection to Preston,and to the right for Ormskirk. Black Five No.**45305** dashes past Burscough Bridge with the Lancastrian Rail Tour for the Locomotive Club of Great Britain on April 6th 1968.

Brian Barlow

(*Lower*) The Orangemens Specials on July 12th provided a busy day for Southport with workings from Liverpool.Fowler 2-6-4 tank No.**42374** of Springs Branch shed,has arrived with one of the specials,and waits in London Street excursion platforms after having had its train removed on 12/7/65.

Brian Barlow.

Bolton to Southport with 43010

Broken valve spindles could never said to be commonplace, but such an occurrence on Ivatt Class 4MT No **43010** put her completely out of action as we approached Parbold with our Boston to Southport special. The noise on the footplate as the valve spindle failed was manifested by a loud bang, accompanied by a continuous rattling sound, which was transmitted to the reversing wheel. The view here shows the errant loco whilst working in the Peterborough area on the 6th August 1960.   *N. L. Browne*

faces from the passengers as they started their day of fun by the seaside. There were some even happier faces from some of the youngsters who asked if they could come up into the cab to have a look on the footplate when we responded with a positive "yes". The following day, I was marked for the same job, with the same engine, No.**43010**, but another much older driver, Ozzie Leigh. Regrettably, Ozzie lacked the sensitivity that I had enjoyed the day previous, and not only that, was somewhat heavy handed on the regulator. Going up the shed yard, the cylinder cocks were closed much too soon, and we slipped our way up the yard, owing to mismanagement of the regulator, it wasn't long before the piston gland was blowing, there was nowhere else for the water to go. After leaving Wigan, all went well until we shut off steam in order to comply with the speed restriction around Parbold curve. Just as the regulator was closed, there was a loud bang from the valve gear at the left front end accompanied by an incessant rattling which seemed to impart itself to the reversing wheel on the footplate. An emergency application of the automatic vacuum brake was made, and we succeeded in stopping with most of the train at Parbold station platform, but with the last vehicle blocking the level crossing, thus preventing the gates from being opened to road traffic. A broken valve spindle was diagnosed, and trying to move again under our own steam was out of the question. On going to the signalbox at Parbold station in order to carry out protection duties, I was informed by the "Bobbie" that there was an engine at Burscough Bridge, just down the line, which could come to our assistance. However, there was no crossover at Parbold, so it would have to come to our aid facing road wrong line. It was a hot sunny day, standing fuming at the firmly closed crossing gates was a driver with a van load of chocolates. His incessant pleading for us to hurry because of his melting delicacies fell on deaf ears, he'd have to wait 'till our assistant engine arrived. The stationmaster at Parbold was a helpful soul and set off on his bike to Burscough armed with the necessary wrong line order form, enabling assistance to come to us, and of course saving a lot of time. The Wigan men with No.**42557** backed on to us, and at a very respectable speed we set off to Burscough where No.**43010** was detached from the train and shunted into the sidings whilst we took over No.**42557** for the rest of the journey to Southport. There were not many happy smiling faces on that occasion, only glum enquiring looks.

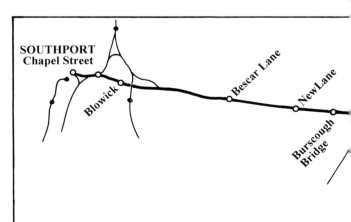

SOUTHPORT Chapel Stre

(*Upper*) Inside the bright and airy surroundings of Southport Chapel Street station, Stanier tank No.**42645** waits, with clean exhaust for departure time with the 1/50pm to Preston on July 27th, 1963. Note the sign to right of the tank engine's smokebox "LYR Southport".
D. Hampson.

(*Lower*). The wide expanse of platforms at Southport's Chapel Street station on June 2nd 1954. Sadly, the area is now much cut back, with nowadays, the inevitable car park on the right. Standing next to the E.M.U. is a Stanier Class 4 tank. *British Railways.*

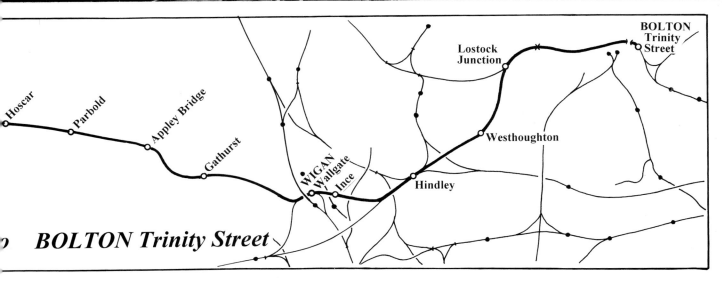

BOLTON Trinity Street

Departure from Southport Chapel Street

(right) The impressive frontage of Southport Chapel Street Station as it was on June 26th 1950, at that period in time, according to the posters, that one could travel each Tuesday, Saturday and Sunday, to Manchester and back, for five shillings - just 25p. Today, an entrance to the station still exists in the vicinity but the scene has been transformed by an extensive shopping development.

British Railways

(below) Britannia Class 7MT 4-6-2 no **70010**, *Owen Glendower*, performs its task with ease, pulling the return working of an excursion from Manchester Victoria out in to the evening sun from the shadowy confines of Southport's Chapel Street station on May 17th 1964 (Whit Sunday). This train, 1Z09, was a regular Whitsuntide working for many years.

Brian Barlow

The Ivatt moguls - a postscript

As with other classes, there were times when the work was of a more menial nature, and for the most part involved trip, shunt and banking work. Signing on at 10.35pm on one occasion for turn 262F, Kearsley to Littleborough, I was told to prepare No.44115, a Derby Four. Reluctantly making my way round to number 2 road where the latter stood, I contemplated another "cold" run as on the recent previous occasion with the same engine. Imagine my surprise when I climbed on board No.44115 to discover that there was no fire in her. Shining my pocket torch into the firebox I could see and hear the reason why, leaking tubes.! I could hardly believe my luck that night. I was down the steps in a trice and nimbly leapt over the four-foot and on to number 1 road, straight into the foreman's office to report my findings. The telephone attendent was somewhat bewildered, the late foreman had not yet come on duty, but it was clear that someone had given instructions for the fire in No.44115 to be thrown out. The afternoon foreman had in fact neglected to alter the number in the daily arrangements book and the board which showed where all the engines were stabled. That night my relief was made complete when I was told to prepare No.43040 instead, what a difference!. In those days, Kearsley to Littleborough, carrying coal traffic loaded only lightly, and on this very night with No.43040 we started from Kearsley with one on plus the brake van. But, after picking up at Burnden and Bury L.Y., our load was made up to no less than 24 of mineral, and on this occasion we received banking assistance up Broadfield Bank. Arriving at Rochdale, where further shunting took place, we were detached from our train and shunted to one side whilst the pilot dealt with matters. On this particular night there was a hell of a kerfuffle going on with police and their cars all over the place. Evidently, someone had been spotted thieving batteries from stored coaching stock, the resulting presence ensued. I had strict instructions from Ozzie Kearsley, the driver, to stay on the footplate that night, a command I was happy to obey. One feature of these 2-6-0's not exactly beloved of locomen was their whistles and the din it made in the cab when operated. Although to outward appearances those whistles were the same as those fitted to the Black Fives, the actual whistle was turned the opposite way around. When the lever was operated which brought the whistle into use it always felt more spring loaded than any other, and in my opinion the sound was somehow amplified in the cab..

The lighter side of shed life at Bolton

Chapter Eleven

As in other trades or professions, the footplate fraternity had its fair share of practical jokers. One such person was Wilf Faulkner whom I fired for over a twelve month period. Built a bit like the late Tommy Cooper, with many of his mannerisms, and with a voracious appetite for making overtime, Wilf was a person you either liked or just put up with, depending on your standpoint where overtime was concerned. One day, Wilf was working on Bolton ballast in Chorley station, he decided he would have a bit of fun. The station staff were having a spring cleaning session, and the waiting room was receiving their attention. Anyone who was used to rail travel in the late fifties and early sixties will remember those large paintings that hung on waiting room walls at that time. These had all been removed from the walls and left, temporarily on the platform whilst the staff went for their lunch. Nearby was stood the engine from the ballast working, and, because the permanent way men involved with the work of the ballast train were also having their lunch, the footplate crew had some spare time on their hands. It was at this stage that Wilf decided that he would have his fun and also play a trick on the guard of the ballast train. Without anyone seeing him, he gathered up all the paintings, and taking them to the brake van whilst the guard was away, hung them all on the various nails and hooks about the inside of the van. Presently, the station staff returned from their lunch to carry out the rest of their cleaning duties before Jerry Naylor, the guard of the ballast train returned to his brake van. There was some bewilderment when the pictures couldn't be found. Whilst they were still scratching their heads as to where the pictures might be, Wilf wandered by quite nonchelantly and asked what they were looking for, keeping a most dead-pan expression. Having planned the whole thing and knowing exactly what was going on, Wilf told them of the pictures he'd seen in the guards van.

Meanwhile, the guard had returned to his brake van to find to his amazement that in his absence, someone had "decorated" it for him. Knowing of Wilf's practical joker stunts he made a bee line straight for the platform where quite a crowd had gathered, there, Wilf was telling the station staff what he'd seen in Jerry's brake van and how, he wondered, could it have happened. Once Jerry arrived on the scene, one look at his face was enough to send everyone into paroxyisms of laughter as the practical joke now became obvious, but with Jerry's blood pressure rising by the second. There were some jobs you expected to make overtime on, but on some others, especially on the day turns, you didn't want to make overtime. Bolton ballast was one of the latter variety, since you signed on at 7.35am, so there was no enhanced rate of pay, except the time and a quarter for the overtime actually worked. At one time however, Wilf would have any overtime that could be got, however difficult and on whatever turn, even, at times, at other folks expense. One particular day on this same ballast working, so far as the permanent way staff were concerned, the job was complete. Engine and brake van had left Chorley where they had been working, and it appeared that they would finish with just eight hours, a full day in other words. Wilf though had other ideas and after passing Adlington Junction he slowed right down to about twenty miles an hour. At the next signalbox, Grindford Bar, he shouted to the signalman, as they passed. "Brake's on fire". Way ahead, the distant for Blackrod Junction, which had been at clear, now went to caution, and as they approached the home signal for Blackrod, it stood at danger. Just as this small train was coming to a stand, the left hand home board came "off", indicating that engine and brake van were being turned on to the Horwich branch. Once clear of the main line points, the ensemble was halted within shouting distance of the signal box. The points were then reversed to lie in favour of the main line, shortly afterwards, the signals were cleared for the passage of an express. Presently, the sliding window of the signalbox opened and the "bobbie" shouted across to Wilf that "Control" wanted a word with him. Obediently, Wilf made his way across the main line and into the signalbox to speak to the controller where the following altercation took place.

"Hello control".

"Hello driver"

"My word, what a wonderful voice you've got on the phone control", said Wilf.

"Now what's this message you shouted to the signalman at Grindford Bar"? said the controller.

"What message was that?", said Wilf.

"Well, you shouted, the brake's on fire", said the controller.

"No no, good 'eavens no, I never said that", said Wilf.

"Then what did you say?", said the controller.

"I shouted, how're you goin' on squire?", said Wilf.

There was a pause whilst the controller gathered his wits together and ultimately realised who he was talking to.

"That's not driver Faulkner by any chance is it?".

"My word, how did you guess control?".

"You're on the branch at Blackrod now aren't you, and all those expresses are due aren't they,?" said the controller.

"Good 'eavens, how did you know that control?", said Wilf.

"So now you'll make two hours overtime won't you?", said the controller.

"My word, how ever did you guess control?", said Wilf.

Needless to say, Wilf did, make his two hours overtime, and kept his reputation intact.

On the Hughes/Fowler Crabs, the seats were of a circular shape, made from wood, and secured to an upright spindle simply by screwing the threaded centre of the seat to the metal spindle in a clockwise motion. Just as they were simply screwed on, so they could be equally easily be removed in a reverse manner. They were not uncomfortable to sit on, were better by miles than the seats fitted to the majority of the Stanier Crabs, and you could face most any direction you chose whilst actually sitting on them. On one occasion, a set of men were being relieved on a local trip and shunt job, the power was a Hughes/Fowler Crab. The fireman of the crew being relieved was a bit of a joker and apologized to his relief saying that he was sorry, but there was no seat for the fireman. True enough, when the fireman climbed on board, there was the spindle, but no seat, he spent half the day stood up. Some time later, and whilst putting a fire on, the missing seat came rolling down with some coal from the back of the tender. The jokers from the previous turn had unscrewed it and slung it right to the back of the coal space from whence it eventually re-appeared. Occasionally, the repair cards submitted by drivers after a days work were a source of humour, some intentional, some otherwise. One of the latter variety, I assume, was "engine and tender braking up", it should have read, "engine and tender brake taking up". For a long period of time we had the same signalman at the West Gate Cabin at Horwich Works. This small signalbox controlled movements into and out of the works yard for engines being repaired, or trialled on the "board side", and for the works pilot which took wagons on to the "Jungle", the sidings from which most of the freight trips started, such as Horwich to Ashton

Moss. Some of the wagons could be heavy, loaded as they were with brake blocks or rail chairs cast in the works mechanised foundry. I don't recall main line trains entering the works yard by this entrance, instead, it was normal practice for them to make the climb into the station yard beyond. Once they had drawn up into the station, sufficiently clear of the points, the train would then be propelled on to the works via "station line". One exception to this rule would of course be the electric car stock from the Manchester to Bury section, and the Liverpool, Southport, Ormskirk & Birkenhead lines which, being electric was hauled as a train by steam locos. As previously noted, one thing that the West Gate Cabin did supervise was the movement of trial engines up and down the board side. Now during the time I was working on Horwich trials there was a change of signalman at this little cabin. Granted, the new man would have had to pass some sort of aptitude test in order to qualify for the post, but as locomen we thought otherwise. Several times, whilst on the trials I had taken engines on to the board side without driver, just with the examining fitters on board. On one occasion, the new signalman had noticed this and duly stopped us by displaying a red flag from his cabin window. When he asked me where the driver was, I gave the stock reply that he had been "taken short". In reply, he insisted that it should not happen again, otherwise, he would have me "transported" as he put it, he then offered me a toffee. Some weeks later, with Jack (as I will call him) on duty again, we encountered our first real fog of the Winter. Now for some reason a brazier had been lit about twelve or fifteen feet from Jack's cabin where he could see it blazing away quite merrily, and so for that matter could everybody else. We returned from the station end of the board side trip and stopped by Jack's cabin, just as he was coming through the door with a lighted hand-lamp which he very seriously and deliberately turned to the red aspect. Walking to the brazier, which was still blazing away, in daylight, albeit foggy, he solemnly placed the handlamp with its red aspect, on the ground, about two or three feet from the small inferno. It doesn't leave much to the imagination as to what we thought about all this. Presently, he walked back to where we were stood with our trial engine near his cabin, ourselves and the fitters on board doing all we could to conceal our true feelings. Now came the crunch, why had he placed the hand-lamp with its red aspect, on the ground, some distance in front of the brazier? The reply we got sent everyone into howls of helpless laughter. It was there of course, to prevent anyone accidentally walking into the brazier! As is well known, the coal miners had targets for coal output at various times. When the target was hit a "bull" was scored, and it was this term "bull" that was borrowed by locomen, certainly at Bolton at any rate. As previously related, the ballast working could make some overtime, it could also take you to many and varied places. However, making twelve hours on this job was not a common occurrence, but on one occasion, the booked fireman was called to account for the fact as to how they had managed to make the job last for this length of time. Now it appeared that the chief cause of this marathon stint had been a "bull" on the line, which had stubbornly resisted all attempts to persuade it to move for quite some time. A few days later, with only a minimal amount of overtime having been made, the same fireman was signing off duty and asked the attendent for his timecard. Somewhat surprised, the official who had witnessed "twelver", made only a few days beforehand, said somewhat sarcastically, "What, no "bull" today?". Came the reply, "No, only a "tail" this time".

As recounted elsewhere, there were times when the unpleasant was ,encountered, and even the gory. The crew of a Black Five were descending Westhoughton Bank when they spotted a headless corpse lying by the side of the four-foot. At the earliest opportunity, they stopped and reported to control what they had seen. About a week later, the fireman of this same crew was in conversation with the lengthman from the stretch of line where the body had been found, naturally, he wanted to know if the head of the corpse had been found. The lengthman was able to reassure him that the head had indeed been recovered about fifty or sixty yards down the bank from where the corpse had been lying. How though had he felt when he made the find was the next question. "Not very well", said the lengthman. "I'd just eaten my lunch which consisted of "tongue" sandwiches, I was as sick as a dog". There were at Bolton, a couple of passed firemen, during the late fifties and early sixties who, as passed cleaners, we thought didn't know their own strength. After early experience of the torture they could inflict, you learnt to treat them with respect, and minded what you said. One of these, Bill Martin, had a huge pair of hands and a grip like a vice, any sort of cheek, however lightheartedly meant, might be taken the wrong way. His technique was simple and straightforward, like lightening, he made a dive for you, and his hand would close like a vice slamming shut in one move. Two seconds later, you were on the floor pleading for mercy, hardly daring to move. At the end of the day, perhaps when you had returned home and were getting ready for bed, closer examination of the spot would reveal a hand mark along with attendent bruising. On one occasion, Bill was working in place of another driver, who for some reason or another was off duty, it was approaching time for the crew to leave the shed to take up their booked work. First of all though, because they were on a road without a water column, they stopped at one of the water cranes further up the shed yard to fill the tank on their Austerity. This particular water column was one of the type with a moveable arm which could be swung into position over the tank by means of a fairly heavy chain. Once the fireman had done this from his position on the tank top, the driver at ground level would turn on the water supply with the water regulating valve. Depending on how much water was in the tank, it could take several minutes to fill up. As soon as the tank was full, the driver would then turn off the water supply, and the fireman would hand the chain back to the driver who would then pull the arm of the water column clear of the track. Unfortunately, however, on this occasion, the chain was let go rather carelessly, the sheer weight of it swung it in the direction of Bill's face and struck him a painful glancing blow around the eye, drawing blood. The engine was reversed back on to the shed road from whence they had just come. Driver and fireman retired to the cabin where the wound was treated. Next day, with a domino school in progress in the cabin, with both Bill and the same fireman in on it, someone asked Bill how he had come by his wound. Rising very slowly and deliberately, Bill pointed to Tom, the fireman, and said, quite solumnly, that he had done it for playing the wrong domino. Suddenly, there was dead silence in the cabin with everyone expecting an outburst, but Bill would have his revenge later, that was just Bill's way. This particular fireman, Tommy Tyldesly, and Jack Ritson, his regular driver, often played cricket with the brake stick and coal eggs. The past-time would take place in sidings whilst awaiting their booked departure time. It was during one of those sporting sessions that, whilst Jack was bowling to to Tom, the latter had badly mis-judged the flight of the coal

egg, failed to hit it with the brake stick and instead had been struck a painful blow on the thumb, causing it to swell rather badly. All this took place some weeks after the water column incident, and to all intents and purposes the matter had been forgotten. Now it just so happened that the day after the cricket match Bill was again working with Tom, Jack, his regular driver having applied for leave of absence. Both Bill and Tom had gone round to join their engine for the day and were exchanging conversation on the footplate, as they stowed their gear in the cupboard on the tender faceplate. Tom was recalling what had happened the previous day and how his thumb had become injured, holding it up in front of Bill's face for him to see. Like greased lightening out shot Bill's hand and snapped shut around the festering thumb, giving it one of those vice like grips. The torture lasted for perhaps three or four seconds, but was enough to bring howls of pain from Tom, and his contorted face told the same story. Bill had had his revenge, there was never anything malicious about it, but was simply treated by him as somewhat rough horseplay. Whilst Jack and Tom were working together, one incident took place which, knowing locomen, could only happen to them. Jack had arrived at work one day with a smart new brew can, the usual white enamelled variety, but of a rather good and somewhat more expensive quality. Standing with their engine in a siding later that day, both men had some tea left in their cans, both of which were standing on the hob over the firedoors. Tom decided he would "start" something and began throwing small pieces of coal at Jack's smart new brewcan. Now it didn't take long before Jack started to get a bit upset at this treatment, so, picking up the coal hammer, Jack intimated that its sharp point would be through Tom's brewcan lid if the bombardment didn't cease. Tom wasn't convinced and tried it again, hitting the new can fair and square in the middle. CRASH, the sharp point of the coal hammer was driven smartly through the middle of Tom's brewcan lid. Disbelief, horror and amazement filled Tom's face, he didn't try it again after that. During the time that the water troughs just east of Lostock Junction were in use, there was, beside the track, on the Up side, a building known as the soda-ash plant. Here, in this plant, which also carried a large water tank on its roof, the water supply for the water troughs was chemically treated. Periodically, deliveries of soda-ash for water treatment would be made to this plant. Owing to its somewhat isolated position, there was no main road handy enough to deliver to the plant, the chemical was delivered by rail. The train delivering the material would therefore, come to a stand in the section whilst unloading took place on the Slow line. Because the train had come to a stand, perhaps for a prolonged period of time, some protection in rear had to be arranged. The rules stipulated that detonators should be laid on the track in rear of the train, and a man stationed with flags at a certain distance in rear would also be provided. Once unloading operations had been completed, the guard would recall the man stationed on the track and of course, the detonators would be taken up. The trouble was, the rule book didn't say how the guard was to make contact with the flagman, and, moreover, there was no direct contact between the soda-ash plant and Lostock Junction signalbox. What often took place was that when unloading operations had been completed, this small train, usually no more than one wagon and a brake van, would move down the line to Deane Clough box and inform the signalman there that work was now finished. By telephone, the signalman at Deane Clough would communicate with the signalman at Lostock Junction, who would then communicate with the flagman on the track. The signalman at Deane Clough would then clear the section between Lostock Junction and his box once the train had passed him. Now it seems that on one occasion, the protection duties had somehow been neglected. The small train comprising brake van and one wagon ran normally from Lostock Junction on the Up Slow line, and came to a stand outside the plant where unloading began. Before all the work was complete, inexplicably, a parcels train from Heysham was accepted into the section and onto the same line on which the soda-ash special was about its business

of unloading. A collision took place, and there was some damage, though mercifully, no loss of life. A quick conference took place as to the best and speediest way of getting back to protect in the rear, and the adjacent fast line. It was unanimously agreed that this would be best achieved by the driver of the soda-ash special, a very strong swimmer, making his way, doing the front crawl, up the water troughs with the detonators carried in his mouth.........! Even in adversity, locomen could be relied upon to turn a serious situation on its head and make fun of it.

(*Left Upper*) Driver Jim Cornwell oils the big end of a Crab's valve gear as part of preparation duties, prior to the engine working an excursion at Bolton holiday time in June of 1950. Fitter Arnold Boulton and his mate Jimmy Baldwin carry out their routine checks on behalf of the fitting staff. *Authors collection.*

(*Right Upper*) Fitters mate Arthur Holmes (left) and fitter Neville Collier enjoy a breather on the running boards of a brake van, just where is not known. One explanation is that the tool van has been sent to a derailment. The date is April 9th, 1968. *H.L. Holland.*

(*Left Lower*) Fitters mate Bill Fairclough carries out work on Black Five No. **45318** at the bottom of number 4 road at Bolton shed. *H.L. Holland.*

(*Right Lower*) Bill Fairclough again, this time, a diesel is receiving his attention on the same day as the Black Five, April 9th, 1968. When the author started his railway career in 1956, Bill was, at that time a boilerman, later he became a fitters mate. *H.L. Holland*

Bolton No.2 Passenger Link

Chapter Twelve.

Early in 1960, I had my first taste of regular passenger work, albeit for a very short space of time, in the then number 2 Passenger Link, at the time, it contained ten weeks work. I got off to a somewhat inconspicuous start with a weeks work, excepting Friday, which was our rest day, on the station pilot at Bolton, on the early turn, the power being No.40202, a class 3, 2-6-2 passenger engine, or, as more familiarly known, a "bread van", new off the shops after what was to prove to be her last intermediate repair. The driver I was marked with, Bill Roberts, was a heavy handed, insensitive slogger, though in the beginning, I was unaware of this. Station pilot duty could be mundane to say the least, so to prevent us from lapsing into a complete state of boredom, a passenger trip to Horwich and back formed part of the working for the day. At this period in time we signed on at 5.45am on the Monday, and the rest of the week, Friday excepted, starting time was 2.45am with the turn number 71P, except Saturdays when it was 73P. By about 7.00am we were backed on to three coaches and were in position at the open end of platform four, behind us, further down the same platform, the 7.18am stopper to Liverpool Exchange would be simmering with its four coaches, in charge, a Stanier 2-6-4 tank and a top link crew. Now I always appreciated a driver who knew how to handle a steam engine, and, likewise, I was always incensed when paired with an incompetent soul, such was now my misfortune. Engines of this class were never renowned for their free steaming characteristics, and early in their lives, attempts had been made to put matters right. Some of the class had larger boilers fitted, just five of them in all, and draughting improvements had been applied to the class as a whole. Because these engines were never star performers, you did your best to ensure that as a fireman, everything was in apple pie order, today was no exception. Boiler water level in the top nut of the gauge glass, a good red fire and the safety valves ready to lift as we got the right-away from the guard. Anyone who knows the station layout as it was at that time will remember that on leaving platform four, you were almost immediately on a sharp left hand curve, often the rail was wet. We set off with a thunderous slip and continued in this manner, slipping all the way into the tunnels beneath Newport Street where we at last managed to gain some adhesion. With the mud taps closed much too soon, it came as no surprise when the piston gland started to blow on my side, indicating the presence of water in the cylinders, and with the regulator well into second valve and cut off at 45% we flailed past Bullfield East box, the din from the engine's exhaust was appalling. By the time we were passing Bullfield West, it was inevitable that the engine would prime, and so it did, water being carried over from the dome to the cylinders forced us to slacken off and run with the mud taps open, playing havoc with boiler water levels, all this and only three bogies behind us. With all this rough treatment on the regulator, much of the fire was being blasted up the chimney. When firing was attempted, small coal was torn off the shovel, much of it ending up at the far end of the firebox under the brick arch. What should have been a "tab ender" sort of a job was being made hard work, so much coal had gone into the firebox that we arrived at Horwich with a box full of live fire. Gallons of water had been wasted with the rough treatment and the priming that ensued, so much, that instead of spending the time reading the paper or having our brew, we were forced into getting water from the parachute column at the end of the platform, something unheard of on this job. When departure time came there should have been no need to put any more coal on, yet so rough was Bill's handling of the regulator I was forced into firing again over Red Moss. You could never win with Bill, if the boiler was too full and the engine primed,

it was the fireman's fault. If you took a chance and set off with a low water level in order to try to prevent the priming, and then came in danger of losing sight of it in the glass it was the fireman's fault. On this early station pilot duty, our Friday rest day couldn't come a day too soon, but the following week I had the rigours of the 5.40pm Manchester to Hellifield to endure, and I wasn't looking forward to that turn one little bit. Along came the following Monday and we signed on at 2.40pm for Bolton turn 108P, the pride of the number 2 passenger link. The first part of the job was easy, as passenger to Newton Heath shed. Reporting to the foreman's office we were told that our engine was No.42563 which had not been at Bolton very long and was in ex-works condition, with a reputation as an excellent steamer. That afternoon I was determined that I would play my part in keeping to the very exacting schedule of sixteen minutes start to stop between Manchester Vic. and Bolton with the nine non corridor coaches which we had picked up at Lightbowne carriage sidings. Whilst I built up a good fire the damper was kept shut, the coal was of good quality and I made the fire up right up to the lap plate under the doors. By the time we arrived at Manchester's Victoria station, everything had been done to make my job as successful and as easy as possible, including trimming the coal to manageable sized lumps. In order to keep the engine from blowing off I had purposely allowed boiler water level to fall below half full, but even with the dampers down it was going to be difficult doing just that, as we stood at platform 15 awaiting departure time. Just after 5.30pm I was filling in the small holes that had appeared in the firebed with the injector on, and pressure at 160lbs per square inch on the clock. Five minutes later, open came the damper with the water in the top fitting of the gauge glass, the blower valve on just a quarter of a turn. Two minutes from departure time, two yellows appeared on the colour light signal at the end of the platform, swiftly changing to green. A quick glance at the pressure gauge told me there was 190 on the clock. With increasing rapidity, doors were being slammed as the last of the bowler-hatted brolley-carrying passengers were piling into the first available compartment. Whistles were exchanged and we got the final signal from the platform staff that sent us on our way. Off went the injector as we slipped our way along the platform, over the sharp curves toward Irwell Bridge and on past Deal Street. Now, on the straight, I could give her another quick round of firing and almost close the firedoors without risk of too much smoke. We were swiftly into our stride, and by Salford, it was evident that No.42563 was in the pink of condition. She was steaming well, from the front end there were four crisp, even beats, showing that the valves were in good order. By Windsor Bridge number one she was screaming to be notched up with the regulator in second valve, but, true to form the gear in too late a cut off. At the end of Pendleton Old platform the safety valve lifted, just too late, I had put the feed on and opened the doors a touch. By now, cut off ought to have been in the region of 30 - 35%, instead of the fifty or so we were running on. Of course, the inevitable happened and the engine started to prime. On closing the regulator, the water levels showed in the gauge glasses dropped to one quarter of a boiler, how on earth Bill could drive like that defeated me. Again, we were forced to run under easy steam and with cylinder drain cocks open to allow the water carried over into the cylinders to escape. Needless to say, we spent the next few minutes nursing the boiler back to health, arrival at Bolton was over four minutes late. Once the four coaches at the rear of the train had been uncoupled we set off up the bank via Bromley Cross to our first stop, Darwen, before an on time arrival at Blackburn. From there onwards, we were just an ordinary passenger train, stopping at most of the stations to Hellifield. One consolation was that during the Summer-time especially, our journey took us through some of the most beautiful of countryside, what a pleasure it was to work over that route. It is regrettable that passenger traffic of a regular nature does not now run over this route, the stations having been closed to passengers for well over twenty years, the line being used as an alternative to the West Coast main line when conditions so dictated. (Passenger services were re-introduced south of Clitheroe as part of a Lancashire County Council initiative in 1994.) After arrival at Hellifield we uncoupled from our stock and ran on to the nearby shed to carry out loco duties, filling the water tank, cleaning the fire and getting the usual two buckets of coal from the hand operated coal stage, one of best Yorkshire slabs, which usually blocked the chute in the bunker, and one of ovoids, coal eggs. On completion of the foregoing we had a little time to ourselves before we were on our way at 9,00pm, all stations to Bolton, where our booked arrival time was 10.32pm. Ending that day, we arrived in the foreman's office to sign off duty, we were greeted by a beaming foreman asking us how we had fared with No.**42563**, obviously expecting most favourable comments. His face fell and he was greatly taken aback when we told him that the engine had primed badly. The rest of that week we had a different engine each day, each of them though behaved in a similar manner, all receiving the same heavy handed treatment. The following week we were rest day relief, working a different job each day, covering for men on their rest day. One thing though which was not changed was the sour relationship that now existed twixt Bill and myself, it came as a source of great relief when I got news that there was to be an immediate "put back", with me moving back into the spare link after this brief excursion into passenger work.

My next encounter with the same link was a very different affair, much more happy and successful when I spent many happy hours firing for Jack Byrne, for some unexplained reason his name was often mis-pronounced as Brynn. Not very tall, approaching sixty years of age, with close cropped greying hair, Jack always scorned the use of the traditional locomens bib and brace overalls with slop jacket. Instead, he chose to wear the boiler suit as supplied to members of the fitting staff, and which were collected and washed each week by a contractor. To complete the picture, a soft flat cap, slightly shiny at the edges owing to the oil and grease which had been transferred to the surface, rather than a locomans grease top hat. How different it was working with someone who could work an engine in an economic and expansive

manner, the way these 2-6-4 tanks of Stanier design were meant to be handled.

There was always an air of tidiness about the man which was infectious, it made you want to do your bit in keeping the footplate clean and swept up and spend some time removing the baked on soot from both side and front cab windows.

When it came to our turn to work the 5/40pm Manchester to Hellifield it was a vastly different story than of my previous experience, passing Clifton Junction each evening in the six minutes allowed. He was a helpful soul, even opening and shutting the firedoors between each shovel of coal on the first part of the job, thus keeping cold air-flow to a minimum. Though I could not know it at that time, this was to be the last occasion I would work this turn, there were many changes during 1961 and the first part of the diagram which took a Bolton tank engine to Newton Heath on the 6.55am to Blackburn, and from thence the 8.15am to Manchester was given over to diesel traction in the form of D.M.Us. The working of the 5/40pm was taken over by Newton Heath depot, often with a Crab, 2-6-0 rather than a tank engine. The loss of a turn due to dieselisation, worse still, the loss of a number of jobs could only mean one thing, further moves backward, another spell in the "514" link ensued, this after just about 12 weeks on passenger work. By the summer of 1961 I was back on passenger work, this time it was to be on a rather more permanent basis, though I didn't know it just then. This time I was working with "Happy" Harry Schofield. Harry carried an almost permanent scowl on his face, hence the nickname, if he did smile it was certainly only once every Preston Guild. Harry was just about as suited to engine driving as a cat would be to swimming,

A transfer from Patricroft shed in the earlier part of 1960, No **42563** quickly gained a reputation as an excellent steamer. She was not long off the "shops" on arrival at Bolton and, judging by the bright new paintwork, must at least have had a heavy intermediate repair. Bolton still had the working of the 5/40pm Manchester Victoria to Hellifield to contend with, and before long No 42563 was put on to that diagram, in my case with not very good results. On September 2nd 1963, No 42563, along with sister locomotive No 42656, another Bolton tank engine, were utilised by Wigan L&Y shed because of a derailment in the latter's shed yard. Bolton new of this, and No 42656 was returned after a short while. However, No 42563 was marked daily in the Arrangements Book as being away at Southport, with the endorsement "T" or "Tick" (the code for engine "stopped") from September 10th onwards. Apparently, some sort of collision had taken place at Southport and No 42563 had sustained smokebox damage. From November 14th, the letter "D" was noted by No 42563's number which was the code word or letter meaning that the engine had been withdrawn from service. The loco is pictured at Blackpool South sidings on July 20th 1960.   *F. Dean*

Passenger tank No 42563

and, moreover, he was well out of his depth and couldn't drive a steam engine properly to save his life. In order to illustrate this I make the following references when all will become clear. One of the easier jobs we had at Bolton was the 5.5am stopping train from Bolton to Preston which at that time we worked with a 2-6-4 tank, usually bunker first to Preston . This job was one of the few trains that called at the R.O.F. station at Euxton, there, uniformed factory police were on duty at the ticket barriers. It was obvious (we thought) from the bulge in the official's pocket that they were carrying firearms, that was our opinion at any rate. Now in order to avoid the distasteful practice of getting water at Preston, it was usual to fill the boiler up on the shed as much as it would hold, then fill the tanks. By carefully avoiding wasteful blowing off at the safety valves, and, once on the road to Preston, it was often possible that the injector was not used until the regulator was closed for the Chorley stop, timings were easy. By the time we were backed up in the bay platform at Preston, ready to work the 6.45am stopper back to Bolton, we had used, at the most, 350 gallons of water, so it was not necessary to fill the tanks until we arrived at Bolton. Harry always seemed to make hard work of it, and instead of working the engine expansively on a short cut off, chose instead to work on first valve of the regulator only, and a correspondingly longer cut off. Consequently, by the time we got to Preston we had used just about 800 gallons of water. Leaving Preston at our booked time, and calling at all stops except the R.O.F., now engine first, things seemed even more difficult for Harry. With his method of working, the engine just seemed to amble along, and to someone like me, I always seemed to sense poor timekeeping, I knew instinctively that we were losing time. True to form, instead of arriving back in Bolton at 7.29am, each morning it was 7.33am for no apparent reason at all, except Harry's tardy running. At this time we had a Saturday evening turn signing on around 5.25pm to work the 6.50pm all stations to Liverpool Exchange and the 10.15pm via Bolton to Rochdale. Spending as he had, most of his time on goods work since his transfer from Plodder Lane shed on the LNW side of Bolton, he had had little opportunity to learn the road to Liverpool, so Harry had wired "EGER" to Control from Wigan Wallgate onwards, requiring a conductor driver in other words. Instead of the more usual Stanier tank, on this occasion we had an ex-works Crab following intermediate repairs at Horwich, she was well run in having been off the shops for several days. Harry was a nervous soul, the apprehension manifesting itself whilst he sat there vacantly, on the driver's seat as we awaited departure time in platform four with a perpetual scratching of the back of his thumb with the middle finger of his right hand. With the early part of this working we hardly kept time to Wigan. The Crabs were easy engines to work on and were good steamers, but when driven in first valve only, were pretty weak performers. When notched up to about 25% cut off and swung into second valve of the regulator the effect was dramatic, and the long travel Walschaerts valve gear came into its own. Imagine my relief when the conductor driver, a man from Wigan L&Y shed demonstrated his ability to drive the Crabs in such a manner. What a refreshing difference in techniques now showed as we sprinted over the flat countryside between Rainford and Kirkby, easily running at 70 miles an hour, with the regulator closed just after Simonswood box. With a 7.59pm arrival at Liverpool, after turning on the vacuum operated turntable, we had almost two hours to spend, chiefly as we wished. After a short meal break, Harry chose to have forty winks in the first compartment to which we had attached our Crab, whilst the Wigan man and I took a stroll around the city centre to watch the activities of the locals as they staggered from one hostelry to the next. Some of them would be spending the night in somewhat less welcome establishments as they were "rescued" from their plight and helplessness and bundled into some "free transport". Arriving back at Exchange station well before the booked departure time of 10/15pm, I was greatly relieved when Harry chose to stay in the compartment back to Wigan. With the L&Y man at the controls we enjoyed a great run to Wigan where we arrived spot on time. Now, leaving Wigan Harry was back at the controls and things took on a totally different concept, timekeeping became none existent. Ince, about a mile from Wigan, and we had lost a couple of minutes on leaving there. By Hindley, only a further two or so miles and we were running almost five minutes late, a fact which I lost no time in communicating to Harry. Amazingly, Harry blamed all this on the conductor, yet we had left Wigan on time, I was exasperated to say the least. We finished the day out, still running on a long cut off, shuffling from one stop to the next in first valve only, leaving late at all stops. Harry was so out of place when any fast running was required, it came as no surprise, when, after about three months he told me that he had applied to come off main line work and join, instead, the ranks of Kearsley pilot link. Unfortunately, (for both of us), he was thwarted at this first attempt to go into the old mens link, a senior man to himself having successfully applied. Whilst I was still working with Harry, we had a late afternoon turn which took us, after engine preparation, light engine to Bolton, to work the 4/32pm all stops to Oldham via Rochdale. Power for the working was a Wigan tank engine, often we were bunker first and sometimes started out of the up bay platform at Bolton. On arrival at Oldham Werneth, after all passengers had alighted, we ran empty stock down the incline, part of which fell away at 1 in 27 to Middleton Junction. At the latter point, after drawing the stock into the siding there, we uncoupled and ran light, up the incline back to Oldham. Next, we carried out some shunting movements in the Stoneyard, after which we backed on to some parcel vans in the bay platform, from here, we worked a parcels train back to Rochdale, departing at 8.20pm By about 8.40pm we were arriving at Rochdale, in the back platform there. Part of our booked work at this juncture was to exchange footplates with Wigan men for another of their 2-6-4 tanks. It was also practice, after having uncoupled some of the vans in the back platform for us to run, now with a smaller train, behind the engine with whose crew we were now to exchange footplates under subsidiary signals, tonight was no exception. Further down the loop therefore stood the engine and crew, in darkness, but with lighted tail-lamp showing clearly, in good visibility, and on a curvature favourable to Harry's vision. As we approached the standing engine, I couldn't help feeling our speed was a little more than it should have been. My fears were proved well founded when, after a belated application of the vacuum brake, we collided with the rear of the stationary tank engine whilst still travelling at between five and ten miles per hour. On our footplate as we came to a deafening halt there was dust all over the place and with the impact, coal from our bunker arrived with a crash on the footplate. We descended our steps to survey the damage and enquire how the crew on the other footplate were, luckily, they were only shaken up. Their engine, a Fairburn tank No.42299 had not fared so well. Both rear buffers badly bent, the bunker footsteps driven forward, and the coal bunker itself was split almost from top to bottom. The engine we were on, a Stanier tank, was only slightly damaged, the front buffer beam being slightly bent, and it was able to carry on with its booked work. We swapped footplates as booked, ours was now the job of taking No.**42299** light engine to Bolton shed. Then, as we set off, metal to metal contact manifested itself in a continual scraping, looking back, we could see sparks flying from beneath the coal bunker where the rear footsteps had been driven forward causing contact to be made with the tyres on the bogie wheels. There was nothing following us, the night was calm, and a full moon now lit up the scene as we ran at reduced speed to Bolton shed, to make out reports and sign off duty. After a compulsory medical and eyesight test, and after all the various reports had been digested by higher authority, Harry was given a severe reprimand, which I suppose would be entered on his record of service. He didn't volunteer the information, I had to ask him how he had fared. I never really did figure just how that accident happened, the curvature of the track was in Harry's favour, the movement was a routine one and although darkness had fallen, visibility was good. The only feasible explanation had to be, I suppose, misjudgement of speed and distance. Eventually, Harry got his move into Kearsley Pilot Link which left a gap for a driver in the number 2 Passenger Link remaining for some time unfilled. Instead, I worked for a number of weeks with passed firemen. It was during this period that another incident occurred, strange to relate on this same working, the 4/32pm Bolton to Rochdale and Oldham. We had run quite normally to the point where we were carrying out the shunting movements in the Stoneyard , which we had entered engine first with our Stanier tank No.**42631**, again of Wigan shed. At no more than walking speed, the shunter was indeed walking just ahead of us, calling us on with his handlamp on my side. I was relaying the signal to my mate for the week, Tommy Moore. Quite without warning, there was a loud bang and the engine came down at the front end, we came to a dead stop. The pony truck wheels were off the road. Together, the three of us surveyed the scene and we decided to have a go at re-railing the

wayward wheels. We reversed No.**42631** into full back gear, blew the steam brake off and opened the regulator, no movement. Full regulator was tried, we got an almighty wheel-slip with showers of sparks from the six driving wheels still on the rails. Some movement, several broken chairs, but to no avail, those pony truck wheels weren't going to re-rail, we would have to be lifted back on the rails with ramps. A couple more attempts were made but it was futile, in the end we gave up and let control know what had happened. Across the road, a class 2MT tank No.**41205** was simmering on some local duty, the instruction from Control was that we were to exchange footplates with the other crew acting as caretakers until the arrival of the Newton Heath steam crane and breakdown train could come and put matters to rights and re-rail No.**42631**. Meanwhile, we were to continue our own booked work with the Ivatt class 2, the forward working of the 8.20pm parcels train out of the bay to Rochdale. Although these 2-6-2 tank engines were gutsy little machines, they were after all only a class 2, and it was a bit of a climb out of the bay at Oldham, most of it being on a left hand curve which didn't help matters. Backing into the bay platform, we coupled up to the train which had been assembled, and walking down its length, we noted that there were fourteen vehicles. Some of the vehicles were the heavier bogie G.U.V's and some were the much lighter 12 ton four wheelers, but all in all, when the load was totted up there must have been in excess of two hundred tons. We determined that when the time came for us to start we would do so with everything in our favour if possible. We didn't know if the sanders were working, so we decided to take sand from the sandboxes, in the bucket and on the shovel and sand the rail by hand for a good distance in advance of where we now stood, it took us maybe about ten minutes, that's all. When departure time came, we had a good head of steam and made a sure footed start from the bay with absolutely no trace of a slip at all, much to our elation and, even though No.**41205**'s driving wheels were much smaller than those on No.**42631**, we kept to the booked timings and continued with the working without further incident.

No.**42652**, one of Bolton's stud of "Big Tanks", a name applied to them in order to distinguish them from the smaller L&Y 2-4-2 variety, brings a stopping train, probably the 4/43pm from Manchester Victoria to Horwich past Bolton East Junction signalbox on July 26th 1963.   *P. Reeves.*

Railmotor to Horwich

Chapter Thirteen.

In more modern times, the term "Rail Motor" has been somewhat misused and in fact really refers more correctly for instance to those units where engine and coach were combined, or were of an articulated nature, as for instance on the L&Y machines of Hughes' design. However, the more correct terms of push and pull or auto train don't trip off the tongue so easily, so we will continue to call them rail motors. By the time I experienced this sort of work, the only motor job we had at Bolton was the one which ran between Horwich and Blackrod. In my early days of railway service it was the preserve of the ex L&Y radial tanks suitably equipped for this work, and certainly as late as November 16th 1957, one of the 2-4-2's built with large smokebox and Belpaire boiler to George Hughes design, No.**50887** was operating on this duty. More usually though, it would at that time be one of the original variety with round top firebox, either No.**50647** or No.**50660**. Because the fireman was on his own on the footplate when propelling the train, it was not normal practice to put a passed cleaner on this job, after all, at that stage in our careers, that's all we were, engine cleaners passed to act as firemen, and when we were firing, we didn't get the same rate of pay as a booked fireman. By 1957, engine cleaners were paid 81 shillings per week, which is what passed cleaners were paid when not firing. At the same period in time, when carrying out firing duties, passed cleaners were paid at the weekly rate of 163 shillings per week, eight pounds fifteen pence in the present days values. Most tradesmen served an apprenticeship of some sort, and in the same way this applied also to the footplate fraternity. In order to qualify for a better rate of pay, a passed cleaner had to gain one year of firing experience. Expressed in railway terms, this amounted to 287 actual firing turns, and a firing turn was deemed to be a firing turn when of two hours minimum duration. On attaining this first years experience the effect in rate of pay was dramatic, when not firing, a passed cleaner was paid 168 shillings per week, and when firing was paid 178 shillings and sixpence. It could, and did, in my case take four years to become a booked fireman, you were then (1960) paid 205 shillings per week, ten pounds and five pence. By the time 1959 had arrived you could say that with a little over two years firing turns under my belt I'd a fair amount of experience. During the early Spring of that year, still a passed cleaner, having signed on "spare" at 4.00am, the fireman for the early rail motor had failed to turn in. The Running Shift Foreman, Jack Coare, said nothing to the driver, and put me on the job. Later on, during the mornings work, it accidentally slipped out that I was still only a passed cleaner, the driver, Albert Hampson, wasn't pleased. On signing off some hard words were passed to the day Foreman, chiefly that this shouldn't happen again. With our fairly newly acquired B.R. Standard class 2 No.**84019** we had a fairly uneventful morning, the only difficulty that day was preventing her from priming, something which at that time No.**84019** was susceptible to, there was nothing hard about the working of the motor. Some time later than this first experience, and now of course a booked fireman, the rail motor was extended to work to Chorley, a couple of trips were made in each direction and there were still trips in addition just between Blackrod and Horwich connecting with the main line. Not long after this extension of the working I was marked for a weeks work with George Ashworth, a spare man at the time, our engine on this occasion was another member of the class, No.**84014**. On one of the extended trips we were propelling the train back to Horwich from Chorley, it being the last of the two trips. We had run normally to the point where

George, controlling things from the coach end, had shut off steam, in order for us to comply with the speed restriction over the junction on to the Horwich branch at Blackrod. From there we trundled easily at about twenty miles an hour round the curve to Loco Junction where the regulator was opened again for the climb to Horwich station. We accelerated smartly up the bank to a brisk 38 miles an hour with full first valve of the regulator and about 30% cut off on the sector plate. On this second trip from Chorley there was usually a standing train in the platform road at Horwich, so the home signal was kept, very properly at danger until the signalman had seen that the train had slowed in response. The routine then was that the home signal would be pulled off slowly, and a green flag would be displayed from the window of the signalbox indicating the presence of a train in the platform, block regulation 5, station or junction ahead blocked. As we approached the home signal George still had not shut off steam, so I crossed to the fireman's side of the footplate to see if the peg was still at danger, IT WAS. Almost precisely at that moment, off went the steam and on went the brakes, WITH VIGOUR, just as George's driving compartment was about to pass the signal which went slowly to clear. Out came the green flag from the cabin, reminding us of the standing train in the platform. We lurched our way madly over the points, snaking first right then left in quick succession and much faster than normal, somehow managing to stay on the road. Once I'd bedded the engine down on the platform I was dying to find out from George what the heck had been going on in his driving cab on that trip. I made my way the short distance along the platform to make the inquiry. The story was this. Whilst we were climbing the bank to Horwich, George had been distracted by the conversation he was having with Jimmy, the foreman from the goods warehouse at Horwich who was travelling with him, and had in fact boarded the train at Chorley. As if that was not sufficient, whilst climbing the bank from Blackrod, and at some distance from the home signal, which, as noted stood at danger, George spotted a seagull stood on the end of a sleeper on the road along which we were travelling. Now it occurred to George that if the seagull remained where it was, no good would come of it. Just as the thought crossed his mind, he chanced to look up and saw, almost directly in front of him the home board, as its arm rose to clear accompanied by the green flag from the cabin, all of which brought his concentration back. Well, at least we arrived safely, but I never found out if the seagull moved or not, or if it was just a tall story. One thing that was a certainty however, was that on this job, whilst propelling the train bunker first toward Horwich, the fireman, on his own on the footplate could work the engine as he chose. With their five foot diameter driving wheels, these little class 2's would accelerate quite quickly. If you made a determined start from Chorley, a speed of 66 miles per hour could be attained by the point where steam was shut off for the stop at Adlington to be made. I tried on many occasions to get a better speed, but never succeeded in so doing. Coupling up to passenger trains could be difficult, the motor stock was no exception. Authority decreed that the procedure must always be, buffer up to the stock, place engine shackle on coach drawhook. Screw shackle up fully, then release one full turn of the screw in order to allow some flexibility. Finally, couple up vacuum and steam heating pipes. All this was fine for those who didn't have to do it, and on the rail motor there was an additional vacuum pipe to couple up, the one which enabled the driver to control the regulator from the driving compartment at the opposite end of the train. A further incumbrance was the electrical cabling which operated the bell system on the footplate and in the driving compartment, enabling instructions to be passed from driver to fireman with a special bell-code. From the foregoing it will be realised that there was not much room between engine and coach. In fact, what actually happened was that the engine was stopped short so that the engine and coach buffers did not quite come into contact. the fireman then coupled up all the various pipes and connections, and finally, once this had been done, the engine was buffered up to the stock and the shackle placed on the coach hook as previously described. On another occasion on this same job, Jack Hartley and I had run as normal leaving the shed at 5.15am to Horwich via Blackrod Junction, we backed on to the usual two coach set in the siding at Horwich station. We stopped short as related so that I could couple up. Jack then left the footplate and walked back to the driving compartment to take off the hand brake, and I went back on the footplate, on this occasion it was No.**84013**. It was still pitch dark, we were the only ones about save for the signalman a couple of hundred yards away, the gas lamps on the station platform were still un-lit. Presently, as I blew vacuum there was a loud thump from just in front of me as the dummy came off for us to draw out of the siding prior to setting back into the platform road. There were two distinct rings on the bell indicating that Jack was ready from the coach end, so I released the graduable steam brake on the engine, we moved forward about a yard then the vacuum brakes went on fully, the gauge showing nil. "Now what", I thought, trying the large ejector, nothing doing. Swiftly I descended the steps, I looked at the coaches and there was a gap larger than there ought to have been between them and the engine. "OH NO", I had forgotten to put the engine shackle on the coach hook. The vacuum pipe was completely pulled off the coach and the steam heating pipe had suffered a similar fate on the engine. The only pipe which remained intact was the one which controlled the operation of the regulator from the driving compartment, though this was stretched out like so much elastic. By this time, Jack had arrived on the scene from his driving cab and the language was somewhat colourful to say the least, though for the most part good natured. That day, the only thing the passengers knew about was the lack of heating in their compartments, but nothing about previous happenings. We still managed to complete our days work without running round at the end of each trip. Had we done so on each occasion, delay would have resulted. The only brake we had at our disposal was the engine's steam brake, the automatic vacuum brake having been rendered inoperable. The biggest difficulty that day was explaining to the fitting staff on our return to shed how the steam heating connection was in such a state. Most embarrassing of all was living it down over the next few weeks, everyone at the shed seemed to know.

Before you can say "Jack Robinson". Jack climbs aboard No.**84019** at Horwich ready for another trip to Blackrod. The date of the photo is uncertain, but thought to be around 1960/1. At that time Jack was a regular on this working, here, pictured on his final day's work prior to retirement.   *courtesy Mrs.R.Collier*

After a spell of duty on the motor, No.**84014** has crossed from the Up Main to the Down Main, in preparation for running on to Bolton shed near to Burnden Junction signalbox, circa 1960. This was the second loco of the class to be allocated to Bolton, arriving in February 1959 from Lees (26E) Oldham.   *J.Houghton.*

(*above*) Although Stanier Class 4 tank No.**42484** of Bolton shed is conveying empty carriages for Horwich, the headlamps displayed are actually those for a class "E" part vacuum fitted freight train. The train is pictured approaching Horwich Fork junction on Saturday September 18th 1965. *Chris Spring*

Prior to cessation of the Horwich, Blackrod & Chorley motor service, the stock used was serviced at Bolton rather than Horwich. The motor unit was then collected at Bolton by the next turn, and, as depicted here in this photo was then propelled to Horwich. BR Standard Class 2 2-6-2 tank No.**84025** is signalled on to the branch at Horwich Fork Junction at the start of the final week of this service on Monday September 20th 1965.
Chris. Spring

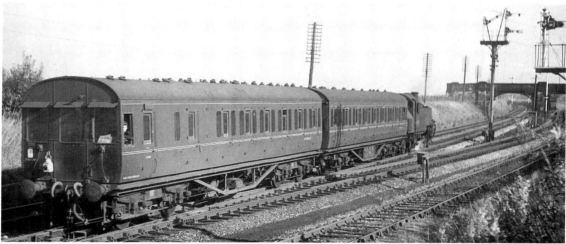

Horwich

Fork

Junction

On the same day and at the same location as the previous photograph but looking in the opposite direction towards Horwich Fork Junction signalbox, No.**84025** has slowed in order to negotiate the curve on to the fork line. *Chris. Spring.*

Rail motor No **10600** at Blackrod. The driver is John Tommy Lord, known at Bolton as "Lord Asta". He was particularly good at persuading his firemen to give up smoking, frequently asking them "Ast' a tab" ?????
F. Dean

Blackrod

Operating the "Motor" for the last time on this service, No.**84025** rounds the curve on to the Down Main line at Blackrod Junction, en route to Chorley with the 4/57pm working from Horwich on September 24th, 1965.
P.E. Baughan.

The main line station at Blackrod on July 5th 1963 looking toward Chorley. Passengers used the footbridge at the end of the platform to transfer to the motor service to Horwich.
D. Hampson.

With the arrival of No.**84019** in April 1958 from Lees (26E), Bolton received its first allocation from the BR Standard classes. During the same month, No.50660, one of Bolton's last two motor fitted ex L&Y 2-4-2 tanks had been withdrawn, leaving only one example to keep the Horwich - Blackrod service going, hence the arrival of No.84019. On July 10th 1963, No.84019 is almost ready to depart for Blackrod with the 4/51 service. To the rear, Stanier 2-6-4 tank No.**42652** waits with the 4/54 to Bolton.

Chris Spring

After spending most of its day on the station pilot at Bolton, ex.L&Y class 2P, No.**50850**, will have ambled to Horwich works, collected a stores van, and backed on to the three coaches awaiting it in the platform road at Horwich station. Now ready to work the 4/54pm to Bolton calling at Lostock Junction. Not fitted for rail motor operation, No.50850 was built with longer side tanks, and four tonnes coal capacity. Often, these varients were dubbed, big bunker tanks. No date for this homely little scene, but in all probability the year will be 1959 when 50850 was used a good deal on this turn. *John E. Porter.*

With only a few days to go before the ending of the motor service B.R. Standard 2-6-2 class 2 No.**84025** is almost ready to depart from Horwich with the 4/57pm to Blackrod and Chorley on September 20th 1965.

Chris Spring

Travellers arriving by train for Horwich works were faced with a good ten minute walk from the terminus. As can be seen from the accompanying map, the works boundary went right up to the line from Blackrod. The "board side" fence, and its accompanying length of track just inside the works boundary ran parallel to the branch which carried on past the connection to the works, under the bridge carrying Chorley New Road (A673) and approx in 500 yards terminated in buffers at the platform end by Lea Lane near to Horwich Town Centre. The two exits/entrances for rail traffic were connected by a spur, which we called "the board side" effectively creating a triangle on which it was possible to turn one's engine if required. Engines for repair entered the works engine first at Horwich Loco Junction at the foot of the plan, whilst trains for the works were propelled in at the "Station Line" entrance at the top of the plan, having been hauled sufficiently far enough into the goods yard by the station to clear the points. The extensive carriage sidings covered an area to the left of the branch, almost from Loco Junction, for most of the way up the bank.

HORWICH WORKS
LMS / British Railways

(below) The layout of Horwich Works reproduced here is based on a drawing initially prepared by the LMS Chief Engineer's Department following proposals to alter several of the sidings in connection with the mechanisation of the Foundry, c.1949.

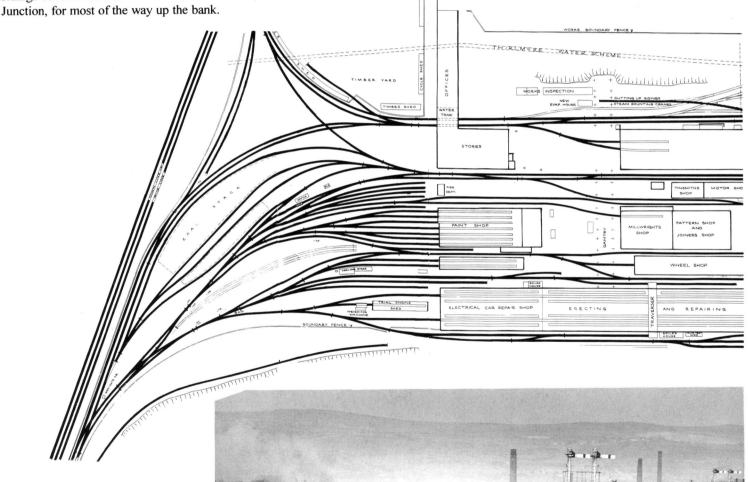

B.R. Standard Class 2MT 2-6-2 Tank No.**84019** propels the two coach rail motor set past Horwich Loco Junction on October 1st 1964. The two roads on the right lead to and from Horwich works via its West Gate signalbox, and rise on a steeper gradient than the main line to Horwich station. Engines for the works used this entry. In front of the leading coach of the motor can be seen one of the carriage sheds, by this time, used for wagon storage.   *Peter Fitton.*

Carrying a BR emblem yet still with its LMS numbering, No.**11368** carries out shunting movements at Horwich in August 1958 with driver Fred Smith at the controls. *F.Dean*

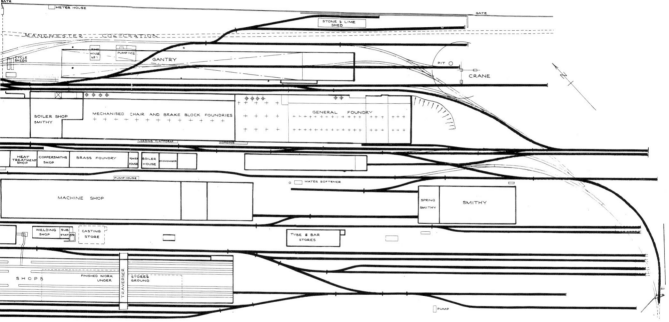

The Horwich trial engines were an essential feature of Bolton's power demands, many seemed to be around for weeks before returning to their own depot, the Crabs were no exception. They were marvellous engines and handled both passenger and freight equally well. One drawback was their relatively low working pressure, which, if it dropped below about 160psi meant you were struggling to keep the brakes off. Standing just in front of the coal stage at Horwich, No.**42870** awaits her front shackle and the completion of painting on March 25th 1961.
Roy Panting.

Standing by the weighing machine, in August 1958, works shunter No.**11304** carries a simple steam brake, so suitable for this sort of use. The loco has the later form of smokebox fastening.   *F. Dean.*

In shining black finish, repairs to Derby Four No.**44339** are not quite complete as she stands near the Horwich coal stage in front of 'Austin' No.**49598**. The elbowed steam pipe which will supply exhaust steam to the exhaust injector lies on the framework by the side of the smokebox. The front shackle has yet to be fitted in this September 1953 scene.   *J. Davenport.*

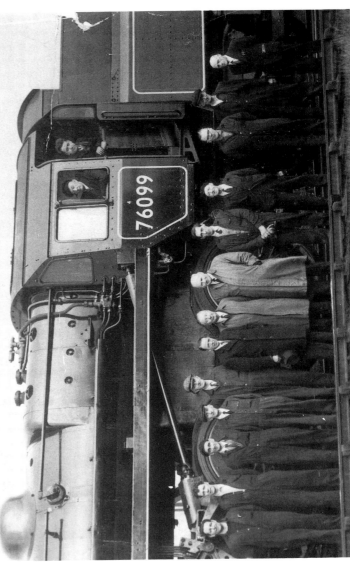

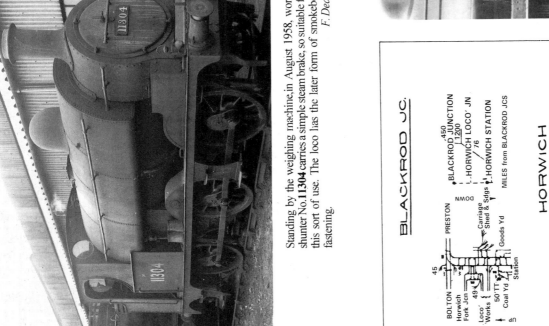

Posing for her official photograph is B.R. Standard Class 4 No.**76099**, the last new steam locomotive to be built at Horwich. From left to right of the group responsible for final tests and adjustments the personnel are: L. Turnbull, E. Smethurst, A. Bailey, W. Pendlebury, O. Davies, E. Brown, G. Fisher, A. Garnett, E. Spencer, W. Fairbrother, J. Sale, H. Bebbington and Mr J. Caunce the Superintendent. On the footplate are, seated, driver Ernie Worrall and fireman Granville Walmsley. The date, October 29th 1957.

courtesy J.G. Walmsley.

Alongside the Erecting & Repair Shop

(*Left Upper*) Waiting outside the erecting shops, No.**44275** looks to be just ex. works. A closer look though reveals smokebox ash on the footplating beneath smokebox door and the general dust and boiler streaks suggest that she has probably been returned to factory whilst still on trial at Bolton, for a problem to be put right on Saturday March 25th 1961.   *Roy Panting.*

(*Right Upper*) The Horwich Crabs retained the distinctive L&Y looks and remained virtually unaltered right to the end. Indeed, in some circles they were referred to as L&Y 2-6-0s. Where operating conditions decreed it, some were fitted with B.R. A.W.S., this was about the only difference. A few, one of which was No.**42715**, were fitted with lift up firebox doors . When in place, it was possible to fire over the top of the device before lifting a catch which allowed a top, ventilated door to drop down completing the contraption. Many of them were fitted with screw action damper handles almost identical with those on the L&Y "A" classes, whilst some later ones had a pull out handle fitted with a ratchet and sprung securing pin. No.**42847** (9G) is withdrawn from service outside the erecting shops at Horwich on Sunday September 16th 1962.   *P. Claxton.*

(*Left*) Only five of the Crabs were selected for experimental work using Lentz Rotary Cam Poppet Valve Gear in 1931 and some tests with indicating shelters fixed were undertaken. The same five locos. Nos.42818, 42822, 42824, 42825 and, pictured here, No.**42829** were further altered in 1953, this time using Reidinger Poppet Valve Gear. The re-builds were amongst early withdrawals, just nine years later. It was difficult to imagine the steam era without the Crabs, I grew up with them, and Horwich. Some did last almost until the end of steam, 1967 in fact, No.42942 is credited as the last one to go. No.42829 is shown out of service, outside the erecting shops at Horwich on Sunday September 16th 1962.   *P. Claxton.*

Cutting up of engines at Horwich was not confined to L&Y types. Standing near the boiler shop on the scrap road, Jubilee Class 6P No.**45559** *British Columbia* is a sad site. Minus her tender she has almost reached the end, and now awaits the cutters torch amidst a pile of bits and pieces from other locos. The date is January 21st 1963.   *P. Claxton.*

Some Patriot class locos also met their fate at Horwich. Two of them are seen here in the works yard near to the station line, they are No.**45507** *Royal Tank Corps* and No.**45518** *Bradshaw* both of which had arrived from Lancaster Green Ayre and were photographed on January 21st 1963.   *P. Claxton.*

Six years after this photograph was taken, Horwich was busy cutting up main line express engines as in the two scenes above, yet here, Horwich was affording repairs to a veteran of 1885.! Carrying the number 925, this loco minus a pair of driving wheels was taken out of service around 1910, and is probably one of a batch built by Sharp Stewarts during 1885. The unit will be returned to service once again as a stationary boiler, for carriage warming when repairs are complete. Note the bracket fixed to the smokebox where the special chimney extension will be stowed whilst not in use. The former 0-4-4 side tank bogie passenger loco is pictured outside Horwich paint shop during 1957.   *Colin Boocock.*

(*Upper*) Operating a special Sunday pilot at Horwich works, service departmental loco No.**11324** built by Sharp Stewarts in 1887 (L&Y No.552) trundles up the works yard from the West gate signal box during shunting duties. Driver Walt Mather is riding on the footsteps, whilst the fireman, Jack Whittle is at the regulator on June 17th 1962.
P. Claxton.

3/00pm in the South Bay at the East end of the erecting shops at Horwich Loco Works on the 8th of May 1964. The works-manager, Mr.Kemp, is delivering his speech on the occasion of completion of repairs to the last steam engine overhauled there, Stanier class 8 No.**48756** of Carlisle Kingmoor shed.   *Author's collection*

Chapter Fourteen

One of the very last Stanier 2-8-0's to be added to B.R. stock lists was No.**48775**, and around about 1960 she was given a General repair at Horwich. As with most engines either built or repaired there, No.**48775** found its way to Bolton for the usual trial period. One morning during this same period, George Smith and myself had signed on to work empty coaching stock from Horwich carriage sidings to Hough Lane, Tyldesley, and No.**48775** was the power provided for the job. She was in excellent condition, having been off the shops only a few days. This particular engine, along with the two others added to BR lists at the same time was not fitted with the usual exhaust steam injector on the firemans side, instead, she carried two live steam injectors. In order to avoid tedious uncoupling and running round, and tender first running, our route would be a rather circuitous one to Hough Lane, part of an area which for some reason was known as "Bongsland". To begin with, we would retrace our steps back to Bolton from Horwich and thence over the now closed and lifted branch via Bury to Castleton. From there, on to Manchester and eventually gaining the LNW route through Eccles Junction, Roe Green Junction and so on to Hough Lane, there, the stock would be used for Summer excursion traffic. To start with we ran engine first to Horwich carriage sidings via Blackrod Junction, where we reversed, in order to enter the sidings tender first and so back on to the twenty corridor coaches awaiting us Once coupled up, the vacuum brake was tested whilst I put up empty stock headlamps, one in the middle of the front buffer beam and one on the right. Successfully creating the 21 inches of vacuum, the ejectors were shut down, and, as a precaution, because of the falling gradient, the tender handbrake was applied. At that point both George and I left the footplate to make a brew in the shunters cabin. Whilst we were filling our cans of tea, a few jokes and laughs were swapped, so we were longer in there than we ought to have been. By the time Tommy Hazelhurst, our guard, had joined his brake, the peg was off for us to leave the sidings. This time of course, once we set off, we travelled over the now lifted and filled in direct line to Horwich Fork Junction and onwards to Bolton. Although

we had twenty bogies behind us weighing about 700 tonnes, to a Class 8 it was a fairly easy load. Once past Horwich Fork, and on the slight rise to Red Moss I.B. signal we could feel the weight of them. But using full first valve and about 40% cut off, we easily got them on the move, from here onwards we could coast along on mostly falling gradients until we reached Bolton. Not unusually, we were stopped in the tunnels at Bolton West's outer home signal, after a brief wait we were given a green colour light for the through road. We had passed through the station yard, and under the footbridge which formerly spanned it when I bobbed my head out of the side cab window to see to the live steam injector which had "knocked off". Whilst I was engaged with this problem, I was attracted to a strange crackling or rasping sound. As we passed under the bridge which at one time carried the booking hall and ticket barriers, the sound seemed to be magnified. Then, looking over the top of the gangway doors, and craning my neck somewhat, I realised that the tender wheels weren't going round. They were just sliding along, locked in the one position, and it was this that was causing the scraping or rasping sound. The tender hand-brake, having been applied at Horwich, had remained so all the six miles to Bolton. By applying the steam brake a little we easily unscrewed the tender hand-brake its six or seven turns. Once we had done that, what an idiot I felt on hearing the racket. All of that six miles we had travelled to Bolton, the tender wheels had been sliding instead of going round, with the inevitable result. Each of the tender wheels, all six of them, now had a massive flat on their tyres, travelling over the viaducts of Burnden and Darcy Lever, the steady, clunk, clunk, clunk, clunk rapidly speeding up as we took advantage of the falling gradient served as a reminder of my forgetfulness. That racket would be with us all day, and I cursed myself for the damage I had done to what was to all intents and purposes a new locomotive. Gradually, with repeated application of the brake the flats would be worn off, but it would be many days before that happened. Just about the same year, there were many occasions when the Stanier Class 8's were pressed into use on excursion traffic.

Stanier Class 8F No **48775** shunts the yard at Kirkham on May 2nd 1968, the subject of the first story in Chapter Fourteen concerning these machines. The boiler still retains the non-standard top feed covers which betray its former WD ownership.   *F. Dean*

Blackpool to Bolton

One Summers afternoon, Jack Hartley and myself had signed on to work the return half of a day excursion from Blackpool Central to Bolton during the "Wakes Fortnight". Arriving at Blackpool," on the cushions", we made our way to the shed and the running shift foreman's office to report, and of course to find out which would be our engine for this trip. Imagine my surprise when we were told No.**48275** which was prepared for us. Looking round No.**48275** that evening before leaving Central shed, it was obvious that she had undergone "Intermediate" repairs. Work had been carried out on the axleboxes, driving wheels, and motion-work, and although she looked smart with her bright red buffer plank, shining black smokebox, new BR crest on the tender and new cab side numerals, she had not had a full re paint. In the cab, most all the floorboards were starting to get dirty, a new hosepipe had been fitted, most of the copper piping on the faceplate looked new, and both dampers and their catches were in good working order, thus ensuring that they would stay open in the required position. Both driver's and fireman's seats were new, and, as with most "works" engines, you could put your food box or haversack, and any clothing not required, into the cupboard on the tender faceplate without fear of it getting dirty. After making the usual checks, boiler water level about half full, gauge glasses were tested and both showed the same levels. No leaks in the firebox from the tubes, or, more importantly, from the fusible plugs. With about 150lbs per square inch on the steam pressure gauge things were ideal. Reaching for the paddle in the tunnel on the tender where all the fire-irons were kept, I spread the fire all over the grate whilst Jack put up the head and tail lamps. Most times at Blackpool, higher authority was a bit keen about locomotive smoke, so I had to build the fire up carefully with dampers down, thus minimising the problem. However, with Jack around you could always sense that something out of the ordinary would happen, and you had to have a fire on to suit all eventualities, and he never let you forget his nickname of "Slogger Jack from Cairo". He always liked to make the job fun, and if there was a challenge to be taken on , Jack would always have a go. With a Stanier Class 8, essentially a goods engine, and driving wheels of only four feet eight and a half inches, you could say that here with this excursion there was something of a challenge, and with Jack on board the run would be a lively one, hence the need for a decent fire. After leaving the shed we backed up to nine non corridor coaches, specials always seemed to have nine on, in all about 270 tons, quickly we were shackled and piped up. After testing the vacuum brake, and creating the necessary 21 inches we settled down to enjoy our tea and sandwiches. About a quarter of an hour before we were due out, Arthur Humphries, the guard, came up to the footplate to give us the train details, weight and so on. Arthur had been guard on the same job the evening before, and said that they had only run as far as Bradkirk before getting block. All this while our train had slowly been filling with passengers after their day trip to the seaside, probably spent up and ready now for home. With about five minutes to go before departure time, the steam pressure gauge had crept round to just over 200lbs per square inch, and boiler water level was out of sight in the top nut of the fitting. Both dampers were open, the front one fully, the rear one about half way, the fire, that sort of orange red colour was licking its lips around the lap plate. The blower valve, on about a half turn sent dark

Oh I do like to be beside the seaside! Blackpool Central's station certainly was just that. Opened in time for the Easter traffic in 1901, it provided 8,888 feet of platform face. During my childhood years during the early 1950s there were a number of day trips to Blackpool from our Bolton home, by special train, always to Blackpool Central, and usually non-stop, a journey which took about 55 minutes. *F. Dean.*

After her Horwich intermediate repair during 1958, No.**48275** was in fine fettle and nicely run in, ready to work the Special back to Bolton from Blackpool Central. We had a fun trip, and an alarming experience, see the story for the details. Although at that time No.**48275** did not have the benefit of the special balancing of wheelset that some of these handsome locomotives were given, I believe I'm correct in saying we nevertheless kept time. The same loco is pictured passing Leyland on a Down coal train during September 1964. *J. Davenport*

A busy scene at Blackpool Central during the Illuminations period. As usual, the tower dominates as Black Five No **44974** leaves on train to Glasgow Central. Two other Class "Five's" are also in the camera; these are No's **44986** and **45371** during September 1964.   *F. Dean*

grey smoke hurrying skywards off the chimney top. The last of the passengers were struggling along the platform, arms full of buckets and spades or young children, faces red from lying in the sun, and the kiddies themselves armed with ice creams or huge cones of candy floss were being coaxed unwillingly into the first empty compartment. A final check with the time and then we're "right-away". Very gently, we eased out of the platform with the cylinder relief cocks open to allow any water that had collected to blow away. A few revolutions of the driving wheels and the taps were slammed shut. Ambling easily down the favourable gradient towards South station there was plenty of time to put a good fire on before swinging sharply leftwards on to the Direct or Marton line in readiness for the short sharp climb up to Watsons Road signalbox. With the regulator well into second valve, and the cut-off indicator on the sector plate showing about 40% we made light work of the climb, and bowled along on the easier gradients towards Kirkham. It was whilst we were flailing along on this section, and just after passing the small and in my experience, seldom open signalbox at Plumpton, that I chanced to look back down our train. What I saw alarmed me, and I could hardly believe what I was seeing. As noted earlier, our train comprised nine non corridor coaches, and some passengers had decided that they would change coaches or compartments. Risking the possibility of a train coming in the opposite direction, they opened the doors between the two tracks, then, with feet on the running boards, and fingertips gripping the guttering which ran along the length of each coach roof, they inched their perilous way

along the train until they reached the compartment of their choice. "Don't look", shouted Jack. So I didn't any more, but couldn't help feeling anxious about what was going on. Although our wheels were turning at great speed, because of their small diameter, I doubt if we exceeded fifty miles per hour. Over the flying junction at Kirkham we went, the footplate bouncing up and down on this un balanced Class 8. Just after passing Kirkham station, a Class 4 4-6-0 No.**75048** was setting off on the slow line in the same direction with its load of five coaches on a stopping passenger train. We flailed along in great style, Jack shouting across the footplate to me that we would be in Preston before the BR Class 4. My immediate reaction was that we didn't stand a cat in hell's chance, so Jack suggested I get some more coal on so we could at least have a go. I piled a load on, but approaching Lea Road, the Class 4 with its featherweight load gradually overhauled us, its crew assuming a nonchalant air, giving the impression that they were hardly trying. A further set back for us as we approached Preston was adverse signals, causing us to shut off steam and apply brakes, the race was over, the white tail lamp rapidly disappearing into the early evening. The remainder of our run to Bolton was uneventful, there, all our passengers alighted, and I altered the headlamps to empty stock code for the short run to Kearsley, where the stock was to be stabled in the sidings on the Down side. Running through Farnworth tunnel, light engine, tender first, there was a most discernable knock from the big ends, something I swear which was not there when we started our journey from Blackpool Central.

(left) Stanier Class 8F No **48357** (56D) makes a splendid sight as she traverses Kirkham North Junction with a Blackpool Central to Bradford working on September 5th 1959. The flying junction can be seen above the top of the second and third coaches.

F.Dean

(below) Even though I didn't get to work on them, the Compounds were intriguing machines, operating effectively, two low pressure cylinders with the exhaust from their one high pressure cylinder. They must have been a fireman's dream when working correctly. With ten "bogies" on her tail, on 18th August 1950, Compound No **41194** passes the impressive signal gantry as she approaches Preston station with a semi-fast Blackpool to Manchester Victoria train, just as Jack Hartley and I were to do some eight years later with No 48275. Preston shed is just about visible through the gloom to the left of the impressive church spire.

Rail Archive Stephenson/W. S. Garth

Bolton "Wakes" in the 1960's

The green liveried B.R.Standard Class 5MT 4-6-0 No.**73014** which arrived at Bolton from Banbury on 30/4/66 was quickly adopted by volunteer cleaners mostly from outside BR. The smokebox plates were missing, so eager volunteers made very convincing wooden new ones.No.73014, specially cleaned and embelished, arrives at Bolton Trinity Street in July 1967, with a special for Scarborough which it operated as far as Wakefield. Alas,the return half of the run back to Manchester Victoria was beset with leaky tubes, though after some lost time, arrival in Manchester was on time. No.73014 only worked once afterwards, on the weedkilling train on. On 22/7/67 she was sidelined for scrap.   *S. Leyland.*

It's Bolton holiday time again, and "Wakes Weeks" travellers wait expectantly on Platform 3 at Bolton's Trinity Street station ready to begin their holiday. The year is 1968, the last time that steam would figure in working trains at Bolton on a regular basis.   *Author's Collection.*

June 29th 1968, and the 9.00am Manchester Victoria to Glasgow train has arrived at Bolton Trinity Street's Platform 3 to take more "Wakes Weeks" holidaymakers off for their annual break. *Author's Collection.*

Trinity
Street
Station

These young people can hardly wait to get away as they eagerly board their train on Trinity Street's Platform Four, during the Bolton holiday of 1965. Perhaps it's the 3/50pm to Liverpool the time and platform are both right for that train which made a connection with a service to Southport at Wigan.   *Author's Collection*

Passenger turns at Bolton in the 1960's

Chapter Fifteen

By 1962, the Liverpool turns were the mainstay of passenger work at Bolton, at that time we were working the 7.18am, 9.50am, 1/15pm and the 3/50pm. The early turn involved a straightforward stopping train to Exchange station where we then acted as pilot, making empty coaching stock workings to and from Kirkdale, finally retiring to Bank Hall shed to carry out loco duties, before travelling home on the 12/30pm, from Liverpool Exchange to Bolton and finally the shed to sign off duty. Power for the 9.50am working, again a stopper into the port was most always a Stanier class 4 tank having left the shed at 4.20am to work to Preston and back with a short trip working - the 8.16am to Wigan and back light engine to Bolton where they were booked for relief by the crew who had started their day signing on at 9.00am. After the prescribed period of notice reading, this crew walked the twenty minute journey to Bolton to relieve the first portion of this diagram at 9.30am. Arriving in Liverpool at around 11.00am this working was also used as a pilot, moving passenger stock to and fro between the terminus and Kirkdale. After completion of loco duties on Bank Hall shed there followed an empty stock working from nearby Kirkdale carriage sidings to the terminus prior to working the 3/00pm all stops except Kirkdale to Bolton. The 1/15pm working involved a Wigan 2-6-4 tank which was engine prepared for the crew which booked on at 12/20pm. Instead of working back with the Wigan engine from Liverpool, the loco was left on Bank Hall shed, and the crew took over the engine that had been left there from the earlier 7.18am working. Their departure time for the return journey was 5/40pm, the destination being Rochdale. By far the most interesting of the four workings was the 3/50pm, power for which was provided at this time by Lostock Hall, its men starting their day with their turn 258. As an example to qualify this statement, I quote one week's power for this turn, July 9th - 13th 1962, Jubilee No.**45584** *North West Frontier*, Jubilee No.**45580** *Burma*, No.**76052** a BR Standard Class 4MT 2-6-0 running in after general repairs at Horwich, Jubilee No.**45574** *India* and BR.Standard Class 5 4-6-0 No.**73038**. Later in the same month BR Caprotti Class 5 No.**73125** was doing the honours whilst on the 27th of July and the 8th of August respectively, power was Jubilees No.**45737** *Atlas* and No.**45681** *Aboukir*. In common with most other turns of a similar variety, running time to Liverpool Exchange was one hour and nine minutes, so arrival was just before 5/00pm. After turning the engine on the station turntable, the crew took their meal break, or as it was often referred to their "twenty" since footplate crews were theoretically entitled to 20 minutes break between the third and fifth hour of duty. For the next part of the working, departure time was set at 6/05pm with a stopping train to Wigan Wallgate, where on arrival, the train terminated and the coaches were backed out of the station into the nearby carriage sidings. At about 7/35pm, the train was drawn into the platform ready for a 7/45pm departure all stations to Rochdale via Bolton. On completion, the engine was run light to Bolton shed, there the fire was cleaned, the coal and water topped up and at 10/45pm, or 11/00pm according to whether Winter or Summer workings prevailed, the engine further ran light the short distance to Haslams (Burnden) sidings where relief by Blackpool men took place. The engine and crew now worked forward with the 11/22pm goods to Blackpool. From the war years onwards, somehow, this job had been nicknamed "Tricky", and in general conversation between locomen and guards was often referred to simply by that name. For many years I searched for a reason as to why the working had been dubbed thus, but without success. Now it occurred to me that it might be a good idea to contact a guard who had worked this turn to seek the answer, rather than locomen who had been unable to help. From ex Bolton guard E.Ormesher, who had worked the job many times, came the following explanation. Leaving Bolton at 11/22pm, the pick-up freight would firstly call at Bullfield, just outside Bolton, then Blackrod and Chorley. Next, shunting operations would be carried out at Euxton and the Royal Ordnance Factory. There, the lighting was of inferior quality especially during the war years, and owing to the track layout, when putting wagons off it was necessary to "fly" shunt them. For those not familiar with the term"fly" shunting I offer the following explanation. On this particular working, the train would stop on the main line clear of all points, brakes would be applied to the vehicles not being left at Euxton and those wagons which were to be put off, into the sidings there, would be detached from the rest of the train. The engine would then run forward with the wagons to be left at Euxton, over the points that would enable the engine and vehicles to cross over to the opposite running track. The train of several wagons would then be drawn into the private siding clear of the Up main line. Next came the difficult part of the operation, the wagons were behind the engine, the sidings where the wagons were to be placed or shunted were in front of the engine, fortunately, on a falling gradient. The engine would stop with the wagons a little distance from a convenient set of hand operated points which would be operated by a shunter or other person and would be set for an empty road. The guard of the train would be ready with his shunt pole, basically a long stick with a metal hook on the end, and the driver would allow the engine to move forward, starting the wagons rolling forward also, he would then momentarily apply the engine steam brake so that the following wagons buffers came into contact with the engines buffers, allowing the coupling links to become slack, thus, the guard was able to uncouple them from the engine with his shunt pole the engine would then run smartly forward into the empty siding, and as soon as it was clear of the hand operated points, these would be reversed to allow the wagons which would now gather some momentum on the favourable gradient, to run into the required siding, the guard controlling their speed by operating the brake on the side of one of the wagons, most of the operation was therefore carried out at walking speed. On completion of all the foregoing, the engine would then rejoin its train standing on the Down Main line by means of the crossover points operated from the signalbox. It can be seen from all that has been described, and bearing in mind the poor lighting, that the operation was somewhat difficulty or tricky. With alterations to diagrams this train at its accustomed time of 11/22pm ceased to exist toward the end of 1963 when instead, the engine on arrival at Rochdale ran light over the East Lancashire branch to Clifton Junction where Blackpool men were waiting to relieve them and work forward to the Fylde from Brindle Heath. It was whilst working the first part of this diagram the 3/50pm Bolton to Liverpool Exchange that we experienced many instances of children playing on the railway lines. The problem spot was a school playing field approaching Kirkby station. On the section immediately after the station, youngsters regularly sailed their toy boats in the water troughs that used to be located there. Many times we had slowed right down to almost walking speed and sprayed the offenders with water from the coal hose pipe. Here was a situation where life might be at risk. One afternoon we agreed before leaving Bolton that should a similar situation be encountered, we would be prepared to stop and nab any offenders that we could, so fed up were we with the situation. True to form, approaching Kirkby, in the distance could be seen a group of a dozen or so kids along with pet dog all over the railway. Leaving it as late as we possibly could, an emergency application of the automatic vacuum brake was made, and as we ground to a halt with our Black Five the small group rapidly dispersed. We did however, manage to catch one young offender, a lad of about twelve years of age. Imagine our dismay though when, on bundling him into the guards van next to the engine it was discovered he was both deaf and dumb. At Kirkby station we left the young man with the stationmaster after letting him know of the mis deeds. That was the end of the story, nothing further being heard about the affair.

The early months of 1963 were exceptionally cold with abnormally low temperatures, so low in fact that there were numerous instances of steam engines freezing up. The worst affected parts were the injectors and steam heating systems. Attempts to prevent this freezing were made. Here, at Blackpool Central shed Jubilee No.**45584** *North West Frontier* has had a lighted brazier placed beneath it on March 3rd 1963. This loco was a firm favourite of mine, I worked on her many times, including the 3/50 Liverpool turn during July 1962. *F.Dean.*

Jubilee 4-6-0 No.**45737** *Atlas* at Wolverhampton High Level on 16thSeptember 1959 was another Jubilee witnessed on the 3/50pm Bolton to Liverpool on 27th July 1962. *F.Dean*

Jubilee class 4-6-0 No.**45574** *India* catches the late summer sunshine as she waits impatiently on Blackpool Central shed on September 5th 1960. The Jubilee lost the small Fowler 3,500 gallon capacity tender and here shows off her standard Stanier 4,000 gallon capacity unit. She was still in great form when I worked on her on the 3/50pm Bolton to Liverpool Exchange two years later. *F. Dean.*

The Winter of 1962/3 was a hard one with temperatures well below what one might reasonably expect from a Winter in the British Isles. We saw the spectacle many times of steam engines having to be thawed out before they could begin their days work. The most vulnerable parts being steam heating pipes where water had collected and then frozen, and of course, injectors. Sometimes a brazier placed nearby was enough to thaw out the part, or in the case of a frozen injector, oil soaked waste was placed around the offending area and then set alight. By the time the flambeau had exhausted itself the blockage had been freed. Because of the severe weather conditions a blanket speed restriction was imposed, on the footplate it felt as though you were running on solid concrete. Just outside the Western portal of Upholland Tunnel on the line to Liverpool Exchange, water had seeped from the craggy outcrop on the cutting face and had frozen to form a solid "blister" of ice some three or four feet across. It stood as a monument to natural forces for several weeks before eventually submitting to warmer climes. By this time of course, all the Hellifield passenger turns had gone, but we still had work in the passenger link which took us up the bank to Blackburn. In the early Spring of 1963, both my driver and myself arrived one afternoon in the Running Shift Foremans Office where we signed on duty to work a late afternoon stopping passenger train to Blackburn, returning afterwards with a parcels train to Bolton. On being told that our engine for this easy turn was a Derby Four 0-6-0 of class 4F, I thought Harold Gerrard was going to explode. He was a good locoman, keen on timekeeping, but,to say the least when encountering anything akin to the out of the ordinary was of a somewhat nervous disposition. All the arguing in the world wasn't going to change the foreman's mind, there was no other power available. Now it was going to be a difficult evening's work, Harold had turned really sulky, so I got on with my preparation work. We had some excellent coal on the tender, much of it in large slabs, which I spent some time breaking up into manageable lumps. Working up the seven mile stretch between Bolton and Sough tunnel on a gradient which in places is 1 in 72 we experienced no trouble at all and arrived in Blackburn on time. Once we had left Blackburn with the return working, the parcels train ran non-stop back to Bolton. Almost as if to prove Harold's fears correct about putting this ex works trial engine on the job, just after Entwistle, on the descent to Bolton, a strange smell manifested itself on the footplate. Now I can best describe this smell as something akin to that when hot ashes from the grate at home had been emptied into the dustbin which also held that which had been emptied from the vacuum cleaner. The contents of the bin would then start to smoulder producing the aroma we were now experiencing. Passing Turton and Edgworth station traces of smoke appeared from somewhere in the region of the wheels on the fireman's side. Slowing down approaching Astley Bridge Junction there was thick smoke issuing from the right leading axlebox. Obviously the axle was running hot, possibly due to being put on to a job which was just a little too fast too early after leaving the works at Horwich. Any further running after our arrival at Bolton would be out of the question. Instead, after uncoupling from our train, we ran light engine to Bolton shed where, after reporting via the telephone at the shed top points to the Foreman's Office what the problem was we were told to throw the fire out and put the engine on number two road. During part of 1962 and the earlier part of 1963 we gained at Bolton a passenger turn, the working of which considering the power diagrammed for the working, presented on some occasions difficult situations. For some time prior to this working we had at Bolton a passenger turn, which left the shed at5.5am, light engine to Manchester Victoria to work the 6.20am stopping train to Burscough via Walkden and Wigan. To Bolton men this line which diverged from the main Manchester to Bolton line at Windsor Bridge was usually referred to as Atherton Line. From 1962, this working was extended to run to Southport, that was where the problems started. Power for the now intensive diagram was a class 4 passenger tank, and whilst the actual work was well within the capabilities of a 2-6-4 tank, so far as actual power was concerned, the problem lay in coal and water shortages, especially coal. Some locomen would arrive at the depot a little in advance of their booked starting time so that they could run under the coal hopper and top up the bunker, thus doing their best to ensure sufficient supplies for the working. Others of course took a different point of view, saying that if there was not sufficient coal on board, a larger class of engine ought to be provided, thus ensuring that there was enough coal to do the job. After an easy run light to Manchester Victoria there followed the working of the 6.20am all stations to Southport via Walkden and Wigan. At the latter station we would often run to the end of the platform and the water column to top up our tanks just to be sure of having enough to fulfill our requirements. Arriving at Southport, once our three or four coaches had been set aside we turned our engine on the triangle there, so as to enable engine first running back to Manchester over the same route with an express leaving at 9.00am, and calling at St.Lukes, Meols Cop, Wigan, Pendleton Broad Street and Manchester Victoria, I have no recollection of calling atSalford, before an arrival at our journey's end a little before 10.00am. Our train would often comprise of eight corridor coaches, some of which were the heavy "Commonwealth" bogie type which weighed in at around 37 tons apiece. By the time we had arrived in Manchester, the best of the coal was gone, and we were well into the back of the bunker by the time we had taken the empty coaches to Red Bank Carriage Sidings. At the latter we would have to wait our turn before shunting our train into a vacant siding. The next duty was to turn the engine yet again on the turntable at Red Bank, following which, we would set to and clean the fire, fill up the boiler and then at the water column, fill up the tanks yet again in readiness for working the 12/00noon express Manchester to Southport via Bolton, where we were booked for relief by Southport men on arrival at 12/18pm. On some occasions before arrival at Southport, some doubt existed as to whether or not they would make it without assistance, coal supplies threatened to run out. Attempts later on to cure the coal and water shortages by introducing Black Fives to the working were really only partially successful. Power for the diagram, which spanned a couple of days was supplied by Bolton. On trying the 4-6-0's on the working, Wigan men, using the engine on its away leg of the diagram were required to work bunker first, or, in this case, tender first, for a part of their day's work. Quite naturally, when wet weather was experienced, this method of working did anything but please the footplate crew and was not perpetuated as a regular feature. By mid 1963 however, a swift end was brought about, obviating the need for any form of steam traction the working being dieselized. Continuing from May of 1963 with passenger work, but with a driver of somewhat younger years, there came the welcome partnership of driving every other day. This was a mutual agreement, which provided George Higham and I, my new mate, with many happy hours working together. An outstanding memory from

Commemorating the last day of steam operation on the line to Liverpool Exchange, Bolton's Stanier tank No.**42663** arrives at Bolton Trinity Street's Number 1 Platform complete with commemorative headboard with the 12/10pm from Wigan to Rochdale. The headboard was removed at Bolton for use later on the 3/50pm Liverpool.
Chris Spring.

Grand National Day 1964 saw George Higham and me working the 7.18am from Bolton to Liverpool Exchange. In this scene, taken by an interested passenger, we are ready to leave Fazackerley with Fleetwood's Black Five No.**45212**, now preserved on the Keighley and Worth Valley Railway, on March 21st 1964.   *Authors Collection.*

this association concerned the working of the 4/35pm Rochdale to Blackpool Central express which by now was carrying the reporting number 1P61. Our day began signing on at 1/26pm, and there followed a short journey by train to Bury Knowsley Street station from where we walked the short distance to Bury shed to join our engine for the days work. One particular Monday of 1963, the weather was quite calm and still, it was also very foggy, and it was my turn to drive. Climbing aboard our Black Five that day there was friendly banter twixt the pair of us, George saying that this would be a test of my capabilities, I wondered how we would fare. Our booked arrival time at Blackpool's Central station was 6/24pm, more often than not, with better weather conditions we would arrive at 6/12pm. From Kirkham onwards we were only booked to set down passengers not to pick up, so departure times were none existant, and the earlier we arrived in Blackpool, the more time we had for our meal break. On that foggy Monday in 1963 we arrived at our terminus at 6/24pm, the booked time, which was something of an achievement, considering the poor weather conditions. The following day though, imagine my elation when arriving at Bury, to pick up our engine, I was told by George that I could drive that day also because I had been good enough to drive in the fog the day previous. That week I drove every day, and although we had nothing larger than Black Fives, passing Treales, the speedo on one of them read 76 miles per hour.

For a number of years, from the late fifties we had at Bolton, the working of the 4/35 Rochdale to Blackpool Central. The turn varied from time to time, but I best remember it when we booked on at 1/26pm, travelling first, as passenger to Bury shed, there, we picked up our engine for this pleasant afternoon turn, first running light engine to Rochdale. By the time this picture showing No.**44779** passing Rose Hill Junction was taken on April 3rd 1964, the train was carrying the reporting number 1P61, which I often chalked up on the smokebox door as I had done on this occasion whilst having the privilege once again of driving with George Higham.   *D.Hampson.*

One of Bolton's "good" Black Fives, No.**45411** backs into number four platform prior to working the 1/15pm all stations to Liverpool Exchange on the last day of steam operation. A member of the station staff has just obtained a bucket of coal from the Black Five's crew for fires in one of the staff rooms. April 16th 1964. *Chris Spring*

Black Five No.**45411** makes the Westhoughton stop en route to Liverpool with the 1/15pm ex Bolton on the last day of steam working on the line, April 16th 1966. *Chris Spring*

Black Five No.**44927**, a transfer to Bolton from Blackpool in September 1964, pauses at Ince with the 15/50 all stations from Bolton to Liverpool Exchange on August 17th 1965. *Chris Spring.*

Passing out Parade
Driving exam March 1965

Chapter Sixteen

J.Markland see Inspector Dunne at Newton Heath M.P.D. So read the daily alterations sheet in the notice case one day in March 1965. The purpose of the meeting was that of passing for driving, a driving test if you like, only this one would be over a couple of days. Arriving at Newton Heath shed at about 10.15am I reported my presence to the Running Shift Foreman, I was surprised to be told to go and have a cup of tea in the canteen. Not one, but several cups later, the official joined me and we chatted informally over yet another cuppa. Eventually, we made our way to a Black Five standing nearby, a question and answer session followed on valve gears. The official made me only too well aware that although we were supposed to be able to carry out temporary running repairs, because the necessary tools which would enable us to do this were not available, it was out of the question, the session therefore was only a theoretical one. Afterwards, during a further visit to the canteen, we had a fairly lengthy question and answer session on the rule book. As expected, particular emphasis was placed on rule 55, the protection of trains, and the use of wrong line order forms. The following day was of a much more practical nature, driving trains, just up my street. Meeting Inspector Dunne at Rochdale station, we made our way to the bay platform where Bank Hall men were backed up to three coaches with their Ivatt class 2MT 2-6-0 waiting to work the 8.45am to Liverpool Exchange. By this time, I was well accustomed to driving trains, and even with Inspector Dunne riding behind me, it boded no fears whatsoever. Frank, the Loco Inspector was now in charge of the operation, so, after consulting him, the regular train driver left the footplate and took his seat in the train behind. As we awaited departure time I wondered if I should make a brake test, that was something that nobody had mentioned, but it certainly used to take place, better make sure that we were coupled up too, I satisfied myself, taking a look. It was only right and proper that Frank should ask did I know the road to Wigan, I was able to re assure him. Departure time came, 8.45am, and we made a prompt start with the job which was a semi express working to Liverpool Exchange and would call at Bury, Bolton and Wigan, as far as I would go. In order to satisfy officialdom, passing Rochdale carriage sidings I made a fairly gentle application of the automatic vacuum brake and noted with satisfaction the reduction in both vacuum and speed, all was well with the brake. This short journey with our featherweight load took us over the now closed and lifted branch via Bury Knowsley Street to Bolton and onwards to Wigan Wallgate, there, my test came to an end, the first part of it at any rate. Catching a connecting train from Wigan back to Bolton, we were nicely in time there to meet Halliwell to Healey Mills with colliery empties, at its head, Bolton men and Black Five No.45239 complete with speedo. Somewhat earlier, during our journey back to Bolton "on the cushions", Frank had asked me what the maximum permitted speed of an express freight not fitted with continuous brake might be. Foolishly, and without sufficient thought, I answered that it was 45 miles per hour. The answer of course ought to have been 35 miles per hour, a fact of which I was firmly reminded and warned not to exceed. Having spent some time both firing and driving on goods trains I climbed aboard this loose coupled empty wagon train with confidence.

Looking back to March 1965, I knew I'd had a successful session with the footplate inspector on the rule book covering things such as the protection of trains, wrong line working, and everything associated with safety. So when day two of my driving exam came along it was to be a couple of trips doing what I liked best, driving trains. Frank Dunne, the inspector was an ex driver, and a kindly soul, making you feel completely at ease, and I was easily familiar with the class 2MT Ivatts, one of which, No.**46405**, was power for the job. The same engine is depicted passing Rose Hill sidings at Bolton with the 12/42pm from Liverpool Exchange to Rochdale on July 1st 1960.   *D. Hampson.*

One decision I had to make though was, how would I would take train through Bury and its infamous"hole". Would I drag them through, or would I let the train shove me through. I decided in the latter more widely used method. Now to the uninitiated, taking a loose coupled freight train through Bury hole needed some care and attention, the reason for this was the sharp change in gradients just outside Bury Knowsley Street station. One minute you were descending at 1:94, and the next you were climbing at 1:94, thus, you went through a "hole". It doesn't leave much to the imagination to see that with a loose coupled freight, unless care was exercised, there was always the possibility of breaking loose the train becoming divided. Once the regulator was closed and steam shut off after Radcliffe Black Lane station, there would be sufficient momentum to carry the train through Bury and the switchback. The usual method therefore was to run as described and let the wagons "push" you from Radcliffe and run at about 30 miles per hour. By careful use of the steam brake approaching Bury, the vehicles would be kept "buffered up" to one another and the engine's tender, thus,the train went through the hole leaning on the engine, and on reaching the level track after Bury Knowsley Street, by gradually allowing the brake to ease off, the wagon links would come"on the stretch" ready for steam to be put on by opening the regulator to make the climb of Broadfield bank beyond.

Only on one occasion did I see the alternative method used. Under clear signals, the technique was to get all the couplings on the stretch approaching Bury with the reverser well notched up toward middle gear. The couplings had to be kept on the stretch in order to avoid a brake loose, so the reverser was progressively let out to increase the effort. On the one occasion that I saw this done we stormed through Bury and made light work of the bank beyond, such was the vigour which Wilf Faulkner and I attacked our task that day. So on this important day, I played it safe with the loco inspector riding behind me and let the train push me through the hole and on the even track, gathering them together for the climb beyond. Rochdale was reached all too soon, on this, one of my most memorable days in my short career on the footplate. The proudest moment came after we left the footplate and the train had started off again leaving us by the side of the track, on the platform. As the brake van passed at the end of the train, the guard, leaning on its verandah shouted his grateful thanks for a smooth ride through the hole and saying he had hardly felt a "pluck" (as a result of mis-using regulator or brake) all the way from Bolton, praise indeed. As Frank and I stood on Rochdale station platform with the swiftly disappearing train drawing away toward the East and the Calder Valley main line we spent a few minutes chatting, the official offering me the benefit of his many years footplate experience, with a few "do's and don'ts" which were readily received. Finally, we went our separate ways with Frank saying that as far as he was concerned, I was fit to drive trains on British Railways, I'd"passed out" yet again, this time I had become a "spare man", a fireman passed to act as driver. I'd climbed another rung on the ladder of the "Footplate Fraternity".

That day in March 1965, on the second half of my driving exam I had to endure the rigours of taking a loose coupled train through "Bury Hole". With No.**42563** approaching on the 9.43am from Bolton to Rochdale, the view gives some indication of how the line falls quickly into a "hole". The date of this scene is March 2nd 1963. *D. Hampson.*

"What's the maximum permissible speed for a train not fitted with continuous brake ", asked the inspector on the day of my exam. As the story tells, I got the answer wrong, and was reminded of the rule that the speed was to be no more than 35MPH. The power on the empty wagon train, on the second half of my exam was Black Five No.**45239**, seen here leaving Blackpool Central for Manchester Victoria on 8/6/63. Lucky for me, at the time of my exam she was fitted with a speedometer! *F. Dean.*

Changing world - Steam's twilight at Bolton

Chapter Seventeen.

Almost coincidental with the closure of Bury Motive Power Depot there came a move to freight work in April 1965 as a direct result of that depots closure and the resultant transfer of work and locos. Many of the jobs were"home from home", one of them was the yard pilot at L&Y yard at Bury. The early turn for this working, power for which was an Ivatt Class 2MT 2-6-0, involved a short trip to a coal yard about half a mile distant only. Once the wagons had been assembled into a train, about a dozen or so, these would be "tail lamped" taken without a brake van behind, and just a tail lamp hung on the draw hook of the last vehicle to convey to the signalman that the train was complete, next stop, the coal yard by Bury shed. There, they would be shunted into their respective sidings, empty ones being brought out. This trip preceded the breakfast meal break, but being only a short distance away, it presented little difficulty. After one day working this job, Joe Strickleton, my new mate and I agreed that each of us would take turns at going with the coal yard trip, whilst the one left behind would cook the breakfast in the shunters cabin in L&Y yard. Joe volunteered to take the trip on the next day, and I would cook the bacon in the cabin, the egg being added only when the engine arrived back in L&Y yard. On this first occasion I was over enthusiastic with the cooking of the bacon which was somewhat over done to put it mildly. The upshot of the affair was that I was "sacked" forthwith and relieved of all cooking duties and told quite firmly that instead, I would have to go with the trip each day to the loco coal yard, a prospect which suited me down to the ground. During this time, April 1965, there was still plenty of work at Bolton with at least 70 turns, some of which were CAPED, the codeword for turn or working cancelled, from time to time, through shortage of manpower. There were also the usual seven or so drivers employed on the Horwich works shunting jobs, with demands, even at this late stage for the occasional extra set of men to cope with the volume of work. Those men who had operated the works turns in steam days had, for the most part been men with either a medical or eyesight problem, and had separate arrangements, signing on and off duty actually at Horwich instead of Bolton. All this, even though it had been almost twelve months since Horwich repaired its last steam locomotive - a class 8F No.**48756**. Two things had also come along by this time which were of benefit to engine crews, protective plastic goggles and of course the provision of the Bardic battery operated hand lamps. The former would have been really useful if only they had not been made from such cheap material. The first time you attempted to clean the lens they became scratched, and after a few such treatments it wasn't long before you were knocking on the window of the General Office requesting a new pair. The Bardic lamps were really useful affairs, the usual gauge lamps fuelled by the rape oil were getting scarcer and scarcer, and the ones about the place were becoming thoroughly useless. Now with the battery operated handlamp you were never in the dark and could easily keep an eye on boiler water levels via the gauge glasses. On the other hand, you had to watch out for the battery becoming exhausted, they weren't leak proof, and once the power had gone, they deteriorated fast. The resultant mess inside the alloy casing was indescribably horrid. Apart from the class 2, 2-6-2 tank engines numbered in the 84000/84029 series, the first of which arrived in April '58, and a brief sojourn

of three class 9Fs from September 1962 through until the following December, it was to be quite some time before we received an allocation of B.R. Standard types at Bolton. By the time we got representatives of B.R. Class 5 4-6-0's, many of them would see less than three years service, at Bolton at any rate. The Standard Fives were comfortable engines to work on, they had a roomy spacious cab, and their seats, especially the drivers with its extra padding were as comfortable as anything else encountered. However, as the seat on the driver's side was fixed, forming a part of a cupboard, it was not possible to tip it up and drive the engine from the standing position as, for instance on the Black Fives. When persistent slipping was encountered, it was always preferable, to me at any rate, and far less tiring to drive from the standing position, constant opening and closing of the regulator was, therefore, easier stood up. The dampers fitted were of a reliable screw action, which would stay open without the use of chair keys, spanners, or lumps of coal or wood to prop them up, though at times a little extra muscle was needed to turn the operating handle which at this time could easily be due to lack of maintenance. The injectors, both of them easily to hand on the fireman's side, in most cases were reliable, and both water scoop and handbrake were conveniently arranged and easier to operate when compared with the equipment on the Fowler LMS tenders. On the debit side, the reversing gear with its "bacon slicer" action was always somewhat laboured and felt "heavy" when operated, though reading of the cut off indicator, carried on a rolling drum was always much easier than that of the Midland and LMS 0-6-0's where they put the seat on top of it. Another feature I was never happy with was the horizontal action of the driver's vacuum brake valve handle. In my view it lacked the sensitivity of the more familiar LMS design, and again, it always felt "heavy" in operation. It was always helpful to have both sander valve and blower valve handles conveniently to hand by the driver's side. For many years we had become familiar with the graduable steam brake on the Ministry of Supply Austerity 2-8-0s' of Class 8F and came to know them as a thoroughly reliable brake. Sadly, although to all outward appearances the brake valve was about the same on these BR Standard Fives, and also, on the larger 9F 2-10-0 locos, there, any resemblance ceased. I never heard a good word for the steam brakes on the BR engine, but, not having experienced difficulty myself, openly scoffed at the idea of any problem, until one day I did have. Spring had descended upon us with its morning mists and subsequently damp and greasy rails. One such morning it was my turn to drive on a local freight working with BR class Five No.**73066**. With about 20 wagons on our tail we were working from Bolton to Bury L&Y yard approaching Bury West, speed was nicely under control ready to stop at the latters home signal which stood at danger. Now in order to effect a stop without passing the signal, I knew that I would have to give her another notch on the steam brake, so I did. The inevitable happened, the wheels locked and we were on the slide. Quickly, I released the brake, and after what seemed an age, the wheels became freed, luckily, the signal cleared well before we reached it. The BR Standard Fives which arrived at Bolton were a mixed bunch so far as their general condition was concerned.

Examples of the class at Bolton were Nos.**73014**, **73019**, **73040**, **73048**, **73066**, **73069** and **73156**, the latter now undergoing restoration at the East Lancashire Railways headquarters at Bury. There may have been others which took up abode at Bolton, but these are the ones noted. Without doubt, the best of the bunch was No.**73069**, she was in excellent mechanical condition, and the paintwork too looked good, it amazes me how the machine failed to catch the preservationists eye. One evening in the early Autumn of 1967 I was "spare" on shed as a result of our own turn being cancelled, my driver had been sent on another job, and I was resigned to spending the rest of the day awaiting further orders. That very day, an accident had befallen the evening Manchester - Glasgow express. At Leyland, a platelayer working by the track side had been struck and killed by this train, on arrival at Preston, the crew were relieved and told to make their way back to their own depot, Newton Heath 9D to make out reports and sign off duty. All this of course, prevented the Newton Heath men from taking up their booked work. From Preston they were to have made their way to Bolton shed, there to collect an engine to work a parcels train forward to Ashton Moss. These then were the events which set the stage for a driving turn for me and a firing turn for a passed cleaner. The engine, No.**73069**, was ready prepared, all we had to do was collect the bucket of tools, shovel and headlamps from the stores, spread the fire, and we were ready for off, light engine to Bolton station to work Ashton Moss parcels. I have no record of the train details, but it was not a heavy one and we ran quite normally to Ashton Moss North Junction where we were held at signals in order to allow the passage of another train in the opposite direction before crossing, eventually, into the sidings at Ashton Moss. By this time it had grown quite dark as we were given the road allowing us to cross over into Ashton Moss, we ran on easily into the through siding line toward Ashton Moss South junction at about 10-12 miles an hour. Suddenly, from out of the darkness right in front of us there appeared a red light being waved vigorously and

accompanied by someone shouting "WHOA WHOA" I reacted swiftly, making an emergency application of the automatic vacuum brake. Too late. Standing just the other side of an overbridge was another train, similar in composition to our own and with brakes applied. Fortunately, its guard had seen us arriving and had bailed out of his brake van as we ploughed into its rear. It was as well he had done so, the verandah of the 'van was completely wrecked, the buffers of it and two other vehicles were buffer locked and partly telescoped, their roofs almost up to the level of the overhead catenary carrying the current for the 1500 volts d.c. electric service. Fortunately, there was no damage to our train or indeed to No.**73069**, our guard being just a little shaken up. I went ready to have an argument with the signalman at North Junction, and wanted to know why he had not cautioned us by displaying a green light held steady from the signalbox once he had cleared his signals, but he would have none of it. His version of the incident was that because we had been stopped on the main line, that was warning enough. With the benefit of hindsight, I was out of order, I was running along a stretch of line which had only recently been re-classified as a through siding which allowed permissive block working, a rule which allowed , more than one train to occupy the section. I was therefore partly to blame. I had though, been most fortunate, there had been no injury, nor more importantly had there been loss of life. It was quite some time before we were released from our train and were able to make our way light engine to Newton Heath shed where we left No.**73069** and travelled home, eventually, via the 3.40am Manchester Victoria to Colne newspaper train, giving me time to reflect before arriving at Bolton shed where it came as no surprise when I was asked to make out a report. Somewhat surprisingly, I never heard anything more of the incident, there had been considerable damage to rolling stock and there must have been some delays, that though, was the end of the affair.

Without doubt, the best of the group of B.R. Standard Class 5's transferred to Bolton was No.**73069**. Mechanically sound, she always seemed to be in clean condition too. I had several trips aboard her down the Calder Valley line to Healey Mills and back, especially on the 10/18pm freight from Rose Hill, afterwards returning with the 2.00am for Edge Hill. None though was more memorable than the autumn evening trip to Ashton Moss when I almost drove her to disaster.
Bill Hurst.

Bolton shed

During 1966 Bolton received an allocation of BR Standard Class "Fives", and amongst early arrivals was green liveried No **73014** on April 25th, light engine from Patricroft, as a transfer from Banbury. This particular loco worked at Bolton until its with-drawal during the week commencing July 9th 1967, having been suffering from badly leaking tubes and seen here on the scrap road at Bolton.   *H. L. Holland*

A depressing site on Bolton's scrap road on March 31st 1967 on the Crescent Road side of the depot. Starting nearest camera, B.R.Standard No.**73026**, ex LMS Class 8F No.**48547**, B.R. Standard Class 2MT Nos.**78028/55**, ex.LMS Class 8F No.**48223** and lastly, much travelled No.**73019**, a one time Bath loco.   *H.L. Holland.*

BR Standard class 5 No.**73040** arrived at Bolton at 6.40am on the 4th of May 1966 from Newton Heath as a transfer from Croes Newydd. This example fared a good deal better than some of the other Standard Fives leaving Bolton for Patricroft (9H) on the 9th of April 1968.   *P.Salveson.*

End of an era

We were now nearing the end of steam, all around seemed doom, despair and decay. Some of the friendly branch lines had lost their regular traffic and been down graded to the status of sidings. Now, a passed fireman, and the receiver of weekly notices, one would often read in them, for instance, "From the 27th of October 1968, the points at the latter will be clipped and scotched to lie in favour of the fast lines, from the latter date, the slow lines will be taken out of use" It was a bit like being in the bath and someone taking out the plug. What would I do, would I accept British Railways meagre offer of what was rumoured to be on offer, a miserable £200 for almost thirteen years railway service, surely, as experienced and still fairly young men, whose service, one day would sorely be missed, surely we must be worth more than that? The storm clouds though were gathering, and I felt general discontent, a white collar career in selling seemed an attractive calling, perhaps even driving a company car instead of a steam engine. One thing though was for sure, with about twelve months to go to the end of steam on BR, our "workhorses" were showing signs of real neglect. Starved of parts, and I suppose, the necessary finance, our fitting staff had performed miracles, but were now hard pressed to keep engines serviceable, so much that the cry "Give us a diesel " was often heard. At that time I was working in the then Number One Goods Link, and one particular week, with a rest day taken on the Monday, we had been operating the 6/5pm, Bolton to Moston freight. From the latter

point, our next train involved a trip to Dewsnap, near Guide Bridge with a departure time just after 9/00pm. After disposing of our train at Dewsnap, we then ran light engine to Guide Bridge where we turned our engine on the triangle, thus enabling engine first running to Ashton Moss. From the latter, our scheduled working according to the docket was to Brewery Sidings near Miles Platting. Often however, we were taken off this work and diverted instead to work power station coal to Chadderton "B" Power Station. The trouble was though, once we were taken off our booked work, delays tended to creep in, many a time, instead of arriving back on Bolton shed at 1.00am, the booked time, its was often 5.25am, having been on duty for 12 hours. That wasn't too bad, it meant extra cash, but on the Saturday afternoon at the end of this week's work we were rostered to sign on duty at 2/50pm to work a fitted freight, Heysham to Ship Canal (Salford). Now to the uninitiated, National Agreements forbad locomen to sign on duty with less than 12 hours off duty. Thus, often in the engine arrangements book the point would be noted that a particular engine crew would book on "with rest", that is if they signed off at 5.25am, they could come back on duty at 5/25pm. So it was with Wilf Faulkner and myself after four nights working the Moston turn we finished at 4.30am on the Saturday morning and would book on with rest at 4/30pm with rest for our own Heysham turn. However, what was written on ones time card was not quite what actually happened, but arriving at Bolton shed later that

Towards the end of steam at Bolton, between April and June of 1968, a scene typical of the surviving steam sheds in the North West at that time. The Stanier machines, both class 8F, and the "ubiquitous" Black Five, were faithful to the end. Captured at rest on Bolton shed looking toward Crescent Road are from left to right, Nos.**45025** of Carnforth; **48392**, an April 1968 arrival at Bolton; **45110**, and with large cab side numerals applied at Darlington Works during its 1965 overhaul there, and carrying a small snowplough, **48652**. Both Black Fives are now preserved, No.45025 at Aviemore, and No.45110 is at the Severn Valley Railway and named R.A.F.Biggin Hill. *Bart van der Leeuw*

Saturday afternoon there was a shed full of engines, it seemed we could have had our pick. Imagine our amazement when we were given just about the worst loco about the place. In her heyday, no doubt No. **73048** had seen better times, but she was now thoroughly run down. The valve events weren't right, neither of the injectors could be relied upon to work properly and there were steam leaks just about everywhere, not only that, she wouldn't steam either. It was cup final day so we didn't hang around to argue the toss, the first priority was to get to Heysham light engine, collecting our guard at Bolton, so we could then get coupled to our train and listen to the football commentary on the transistor I'd brought with me. On arrival at Heysham we were surprised to find "Little Nelly" the gyrocopter used in one of the Bond films there with a notice to the effect that it was being sponsored by Players cigarettes. There was no one in attendance, so we were unable to ask any questions as to what it was being sponsored for. We quickly coupled to our train, 28 loaded vehicles, the transistor was placed on the window ledge by my side and we took our meal break. Our guard who had travelled with us, Leo Swire, was stood immediately behind where I was sat, likewise he was eating his sandwiches. Leo was quite a character, always had a pocketful of sweets and ALWAYS seemed to be wearing wellies. Three quarters of the way through our meal break, Leo spotted something of interest and called our attention by pointing in its direction. His raincoat sleeve caught the delicately balanced transistor and sent it crashing to the ground where it smashed into many pieces. I was down the steps in a trice followed by the crestfallen Leo full of apologies. Although the set was in many pieces, the thing had not parted company with its batteries and miraculously was still playing, so we picked up the bits and arranged them on the tender and were able to listen to the remainder of the commentary. What a stinker of a trip we had, the first part of the job was not too bad once we got them on them over on the West Coast main line. After Preston though, climbing Chorley Bank not only would she not steam she wouldn't climb either, a straightforward job had been made hard

work. Arriving back on Bolton shed to sign off duty later that night I couldn't resist having a go at the afternoon Foreman, though of course, he had played no part in arranging the power for the earlier part of the day, it ended up becoming a heated argument. He rounding the thing off saying we would have manage with them until we got the diesels. Well, twelve or so months later we got the diesels, and for a few weeks they were a novelty, but it didn't take long to discover that they were horrible smelly things and boredom soon set in, there was little or nothing for the second man to do, save keep a sharp lookout. On the plus side, yes, there was one, the response to a generous opening of the throttle or controller could be"electrifying". When reversing light engine into the holding sidings at Byng Street, Bolton, our "new" depot, the noise from the type 2's exhaust was indeed impressive as it hit the underside of Trinity Street bridge. The question was, how long could I put up with knowing that any more driving turns would be virtually out of the question. Re-enforcing that fact was the knowledge that for the moment at any rate, there were no plans for my seniority to undergo diesel training. Gone now were those steam shed days of fitters shops, sandholes and disposal ash pits with the familiar piles of smokebox ash and clinker, with a hint of a light blue smoke haze drifting upwards into the dusk of a Summer's evening. Gone too, the roar as another 16 ton wagon disgorges its contents into the depths of the coal hopper and the noise from beneath as another engine comes on shed and fills up tender or bunker. Gone too the line of Austerities, Black Fives and Stanier tanks, standing guard, awaiting their turn to have firebox,ash pan and smokebox cleared. The start of Bolton "Wakes Weeks" of 1968 would be unlike any other had been, in Bolton at any rate. That particular event coincided with the closure of Bolton Motive Power Depot 9K to steam working. From thence onwards we were to work from Byng Street, near Bolton station, our new signing on point, with only a few small sidings nearby where our new work horses would be stabled. There'd be no more SHOVELLING FOR STEAM.

Just about the worst of any of the BR Standard Class 5's to be allocated to Bolton was No **73048**. As recounted in the final chapter, just about everything that could go wrong with a locomotive, did go wrong. Nobody was too upset when she was noted on the scrap road, as in this November 4th 1967 view, with part of the motion removed prior to removal for cutting up.   *Chris Spring*

← (left) With the end of steam in sight, there is a much brighter future for this loco. Driver Fred Dunham and Fireman Colin Begg take a breather in the loop at Broadfield on the section of line between Castleton and Bury. Black Five No **44871** was eventually preserved at Carnforth's "Steamtown".

Bart van der Leeuw

↑ (above) Black Five No **44728**, a September arrival at Bolton, poses along with a group from the fitting staff outside on number five road at Bolton shed. This loco had been a Southport engine, but enjoyed a brief sojourn at Blackpool before arriving at Bolton and a January 1968 withdrawal. The person on the left of the two beneath the smokebox has so far not been identified, but the one on the right is Tommy Burns. Standing, left to right; Denis Green, next to an unidentified fitter; Mr. Burgess in trilby hat and spectacles; Jimmy Jenks, Bert Peck, Harry Hall, Tommy Truman, Ralph Bolton, Arthur Holmes, George Wright.

Bart van der Leeuw

← (left) The first Black Five to arrive at Bolton in February 1962 from Newton Heath, No **45290**. Driver Bob Wilson is at the controls along with a happy group from the fitting staff; left to right; George Wright, fitter, Neville Collier, fitter; Bert Peck, fitter; Harry Hall, fitter, and Ralph Bolton, fitters mate; Just who the other person on the footplate is

Pictured with Black Five No. **44728**, Bart van der Leeuw, a Dutch steam enthusiast, spent some time at Bolton working as fitters mate during 1967 and 1968, thoroughly enjoying himself, and has kept in touch with the Truman family - his English guardians. He remembers well, along with colleagues, playing cards in cold fireboxes by candle light, having asked to be let out by a certain time, it wasn't possible to open the firedoors from the inside.   *Bart van der Leeuw.*

A sight soon to be seen no more, piles of ash and clinker disposed of from ash pans and fireboxes. Standing over the ash disposal pit only weeks before the end of steam at Bolton is a most respectable and clean looking No. **45046**, a May 1968 arrival from Stockport.   *Bart van der Leeuw.*

(*Left upper*) All the atmosphere of a steam shed is captured in the 1968 view framed by the shed roof. Pools of water lie on the grease laden floor, and the Stanier machine standing firm to the end with Black Fives Nos. **44947**, **45073** & **45260** on parade.
Bart van der Leeuw

A favourite place in the fitting shop to take a meal break and possibly a few minutes shut-eye was around the warmth of the blacksmiths forge. On the left rear row is shedman, John Kilcoyne. Next, Tommy Truman, fitters mate; then fitter Bert Peck, whilst on the right is boilerman Bill Fairclough. The man on the left of the front row is also thought to be another member of the boiler staff. Finally, on the right of the front row is shedman Bill Taylor, perhaps best remembered for his work on the ash disposal pit.
Bart van der Leeuw

The last steam turn at Bolton shed and its preparations turned out to be something of a damp squib. Driver Tommy Sammon makes some fine adjustments to No.**45269**'s commemorative headboard as loco and men wait at Agecroft Junction to work a freight to Dewsnap. Sadly, after waiting for some time, the working was cancelled owing to a strike by goods guards.   *P. Salveson.*

The

Bolton's Black Five No.**45269** is turned on the shed turntable to face toward Manchester prior to running light to Agecroft Junction ready for the Dewsnap working with driver Tommy Sammon at the turntable controls.   *N.E. Preedy.*

End

Two photographs that say it all. Bolton shed, empty and silent except for the scrap metal dealers equipment in 1969. The end of an era, what more can be said?
          both- Bart van der Leeuw.